# ALL-TERRAIN PUSHCHAIR WALKS
## *North Lakeland*

## Ruth & Richard Irons

**Published by** Sigma Leisure – an imprint of
Sigma Press, 5 Alton Road, Wilmslow, Cheshire SK9 5DY, England.

**British Library Cataloguing in Publication Data**
A CIP record for this book is available from the British Library.

**ISBN:** 1-85058-802-3

**Typesetting and Design by:** Sigma Press, Wilmslow, Cheshire.

**Cover photograph:** Ruth Irons on the Glenderaterra walk

**Maps:** Richard Irons. Reproduced from Ordnance Survey mapping on behalf of The Controller of Her Majesty's Stationery Office. © Crown Copyright. Licence Number MC 1000320588

**Photographs:** Ruth & Richard Irons

**Printed by:** Bell & Bain Ltd, Glasgow

**Disclaimer:** the information in this book is given in good faith and is believed to be correct at the time of publication. No responsibility is accepted by either the author or publisher for errors or omissions, or for any loss or injury howsoever caused. Only you can judge your own fitness, competence and experience. Do not rely solely on sketch maps for navigation; we strongly recommend the use of appropriate Ordnance Survey (or equivalent) maps.

# *Preface*

The first few weeks of parenting pass in a haze of exhaustion, sleepsuits, nappy sacks and well-wishers. But there comes a time when these things give way to a menagerie of fluffy animals and enough gaudy plastic to stock a nursery school. A time when you will long for a breath of fresh air, some wide open space and a rendezvous with nature.

The advent of the All-Terrain Pushchair has enabled young families to access more remote areas than ever before and this book details thirty walks for you to try. The routes range from gentle strolls in pretty Lakeland villages to hefty hikes across exposed, windswept fells. It caters for the Sunday sofa-loafer, the perky peak-bagger and everyone in-between!

The introduction includes a general resumé about the book, friendly advice on day tripping with babies, an All-Terrain Pushchair appraisal, a reminder of the country code and an at-a-glance walk selector.

We trust that this book will give you and your charges an enjoyable outdoor experience and will help you to nurture in them an enthusiasm for adventure. Go out and enjoy it!

*Ruth and Richard Irons.*

*To Keith and Linda, without the caravan this would have been impossible.*

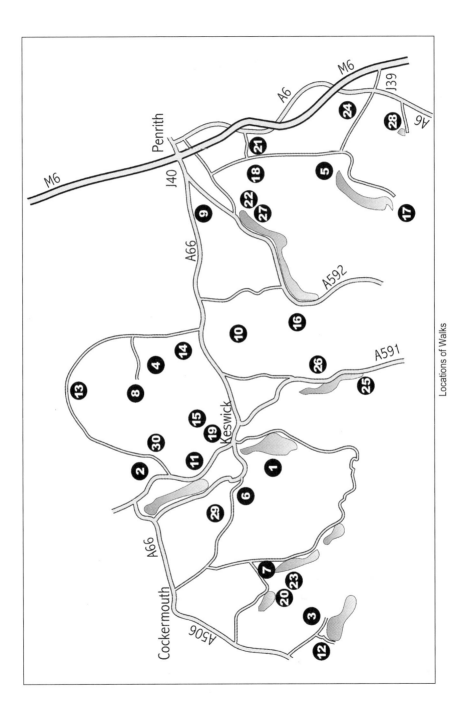

Locations of Walks

# Contents

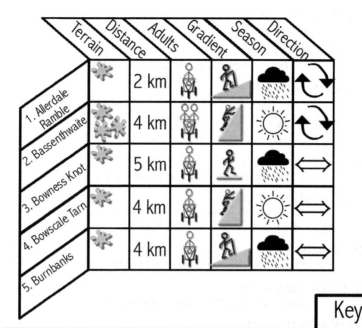

| Terrain | Distance | Adults | Gradient | Season | Direction |
|---------|----------|--------|----------|--------|-----------|
| 1. Allerdale Ramble | 2 km | | | | |
| 2. Bassenthwaite | 4 km | | | | |
| 3. Bowness Knot | 5 km | | | | |
| 4. Bowscale Tarn | 4 km | | | | |
| 5. Burnbanks | 4 km | | | | |

## Key

 Firm ground, some rocks, minimal puddles. Suggested footwear: trainers.

 Some deep puddles or stretches of soft muddy ground. Suggested footwear: lightweight walking boots.

 Very wet and muddy after rain. Suggested footwear: waterproof hiking boots or wellington boots.

 Route is flat or has very few demanding climbs.

 Route requires more exertion. Longer stretches of gentle ascents/descents.

"Lung Busters!" - the route requires a certain degree of fitness, ascents/descents are steeper and longer.

 Route is suitable for one lone adult and child(ren) - no ATP carrying required.

 2 adults and child(ren) preferable - some carrying required/share out ATP pushing on steep climbs/steep descents require second adult to lead in front of ATP for extra security/remote area.

 Route is best attempted in summer or after periods of dry weather. Potentially very exposed/high altitude/ground drainage poor/very muddy.

 Suitable for all-year-round walking - low altitude/firm tracks with good drainage.

 Route is circular. Will require closer attention to map and route description.

Route is non-circular (returns along outward route). Easier to navigate. Route can be shortened/lengthened to suit.

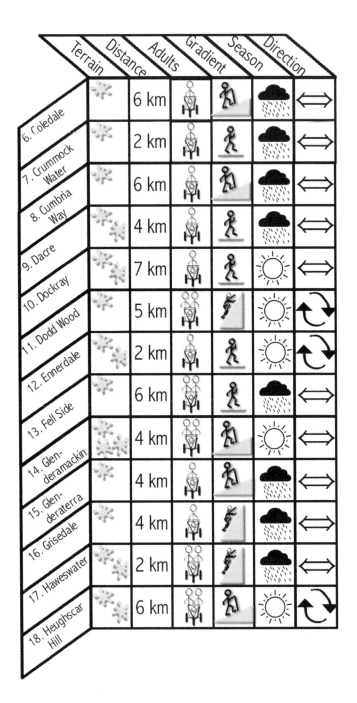

| Terrain | Distance | Adults | Gradient | Season | Direction |
|---|---|---|---|---|---|
| 6. Coledale | 6 km | | | | |
| 7. Crummock Water | 2 km | | | | |
| 8. Cumbria Way | 6 km | | | | |
| 9. Dacre | 4 km | | | | |
| 10. Dockray | 7 km | | | | |
| 11. Dodd Wood | 5 km | | | | |
| 12. Ennerdale | 2 km | | | | |
| 13. Fell Side | 6 km | | | | |
| 14. Glenderamackin | 4 km | | | | |
| 15. Glenderaterra | 4 km | | | | |
| 16. Grisedale | 4 km | | | | |
| 17. Haweswater | 2 km | | | | |
| 18. Heughscar Hill | 6 km | | | | |

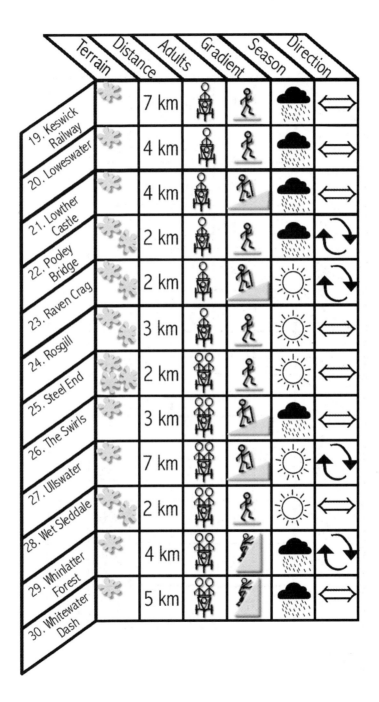

| | Terrain | Distance | Adults | Gradient | Season | Direction |
|---|---|---|---|---|---|---|
| 19. Keswick Railway | ❄ | 7 km | 🚶🚶 | 🚶 | 🌧 | ⟷ |
| 20. Loweswater | ❄ | 4 km | 🚶🚶 | 🚶 | 🌧 | ⟷ |
| 21. Lowther Castle | ❄ | 4 km | 🚶🚶 | 🚶 | 🌧 | ⟷ |
| 22. Pooley Bridge | ❄❄ | 2 km | 🚶🚶 | 🚶 | 🌧 | ↻ |
| 23. Raven Crag | ❄❄ | 2 km | 🚶🚶 | 🚶 | ☀ | ↻ |
| 24. Rosgill | ❄❄ | 3 km | 🚶🚶 | 🚶 | ☀ | ⟷ |
| 25. Steel End | ❄❄ | 2 km | 🚶🚶 | 🚶 | ☀ | ⟷ |
| 26. The Swirls | ❄ | 3 km | 🚶🚶 | 🚶 | 🌧 | ⟷ |
| 27. Ullswater | ❄ | 7 km | 🚶🚶 | 🚶 | ☀ | ↻ |
| 28. Wet Sleddale | ❄❄ | 2 km | 🚶🚶 | 🚶 | ☀ | ⟷ |
| 29. Whinlatter Forest | ❄ | 4 km | 🚶🚶 | 🚶 | 🌧 | ↻ |
| 30. Whitewater Dash | ❄ | 5 km | 🚶🚶 | 🚶 | 🌧 | ⟷ |

# About This Book

The routes in this book are listed alphabetically, so their order relates to neither the distance nor difficulty of the walk. Two adjacent walks on the map could vary greatly in both terrain and gradient. Grading of the walks (from easy to difficult) has been avoided since such ranking is over-simplistic and entirely subjective. For example, which is more difficult – a 2km walk with steep climbs or a 6km flat walk?

The book lets the reader decide which route is most suitable by way of an at-a-glance route selector. Giving details of distance, terrain, and gradient, the easy to interpret symbols and explanatory key gives a quick and graphic resume of each walk. Coupled with the introductory section at the beginning of each route, the walker will know exactly what to expect before embarking.

The shortest walk is 2km long and takes about 45 minutes to walk, with no stops. The longest can take up to 4 hours to cover the 7km. Some walks follow the same route there and back again, so can be varied in length to suit different needs. Other routes are for those who wish to explore teashops in pretty Lakeland villages, whilst some are for hardy adventurers who wish to travel far from the beaten track. Where walks are particularly appropriate for people wanting a gentle introduction to ATP walking off-road, they are marked as such. All of the routes are on public rights of way, avoiding stiles, walls, fences and locked gates wherever possible

The routes are split into numbered 'legs'. The location of each leg is marked by its number on the map. This allows the text and map to be followed simultaneously.

While details of directions to the start of the walk are given where possible, the definitive location is provided by a grid reference. This locates the exact position of the start of the route on Ordnance Survey Maps (Explorer/Outdoor Leisure and Landranger) by way of a 6-figure number. The number is, in fact, a pair of three-digit numbers indicating a horizontal and vertical position on the map.

For example, the grid reference for the start of route 1 is 247212. The first three digits (247) represent the horizontal position; the second three digits (212) represent the vertical position. This is how to interpret the numbers:

247: Using the vertical grid line numbering on the bottom of one of the maps one can easily find line number 24. The 7 represents seven-tenths of the distance to line 25. (On the OS Explorer maps, tenths of a square are marked). Trace an imaginary vertical line from this position.

212: Likewise, the horizontal grid line 21 can be found, and an imaginary line two-tenths of a square above it can be traced across the map. Where the two lines cross is at position 247212. From here, the map may then be studied to plan how to journey to the start of the route.

Ideally, walkers should have a basic understanding of map reading and the use of a compass. If in doubt, seek advice from someone experienced in navigating mountainous terrain. A few minutes of tuition may prove invaluable in completing a walk quickly and safely.

# The Country Code

The Country Code allows everyone to benefit from their day out by paying due respect to the countryside, its life and its work.

☆ Do not drop litter. Use a bin or take it home.

☆ Do not stray from public footpaths or bridleways.

☆ Do not pick any plants.

☆ Make no unnecessary noise.

☆ Keep dogs on a lead near livestock and under close control at all other times.

☆ Leave gates as you find them.

☆ Use gates or stiles to cross fences, hedges or walls.

☆ Do not touch livestock, crops or farm machinery.

☆ Keep the natural water supply clean.

☆ Walk in single file and on the right-hand side of roads.

☆ Do not cross railway lines except by bridges.

☆ Guard against the risk of fire.

# All-Terrain Pushchairs – General Information

All-Terrain Pushchairs (ATPs) have become popular and fashionable about town, and may appear, at first glance, to be nothing more than a gimmick-laden ordinary pushchair. While ATPs may spend the majority of their time on metalled surfaces, they are designed to cope especially well with much rougher terrain. Their ability to do this is based on the following design features unique to ATPs:

**Figure 1.** ATPs can negotiate fairly rough terrain with ease

☆ Three wheels with pneumatic tyres – providing comfort and manoeuvrability over rough terrain.

☆ A light aluminium frame – providing extra strength while minimising weight.

☆ A long wheelbase – providing increased stability.

These features result in a well-balanced pushchair that handles well off-road whilst providing safety and comfort for children in the pre-school years.

Indeed, ATPs are a formidable competitor to the more conventional papoose. They roll easily over rocks (see Fig.1), mud, sand, shingle, grass and snow whilst providing total protection from the elements and a warm, safe, comfortable place to sleep. Toddlers are able to eat and drink in situ and can climb in and out without too much fuss, whilst adults can change over responsibility of "carrying" the children very easily. The pushchair is the only viable option if you are travelling as a single adult with two babies, and of course, without the pushchair everything that is being supported by those three wheels would be on your back!

# Advice for first-time buyers

It is worth doing some research and considering the options carefully before finally selecting a particular model of ATP. Differences include weight, handling, width when folded, ease of folding, cost, features (for example car seat adapter, handbrake, quick release wheels, new-born accessories) and of course, personal taste. Remember to check that the model will go through your front door and fit into the boot of your car. Bear in mind the main way that the pushchair will be used. Some models are built to be frequently used on very rough ground and others are more suitable for occasional off road use.

## *Accessories*

Any pushchair with pneumatic tyres, a strong frame and a good raincover will safely and comfortably handle the routes in this book. Additional useful accessories include a sunshade and a luggage tray. Buggy boards are not recommended in any situation because the front wheels are difficult to lift and this affects the handling and steering over rough ground. A buggy board also carries the risk of the pushchair tipping over backwards; so if you must use one, be careful!

Most All-Terrain Pushchairs have a fixed front wheel because they are so well balanced and can be guided by a light touch of the handle. Others have a swivel wheel at the front that may or may not be lockable. The best performance from these pushchairs is obtained when the wheel is free to swivel about town and locked when travelling over rough ground.

**Walking with your new-born baby**

Carrycots and specific new-born adapters can be purchased as optional extras for some pushchairs. These arrive with the warning that it is dangerous to jolt or shake a young baby under any circumstance. Exactly when a baby is ready to travel over rough ground is open to debate and will vary according to the model that you have chosen. As a rule, the further the seat reclines and the more the head is supported, the younger the infant that can be accommodated. Pushchairs that do not have reclining seats are only suitable for babies over six months of age. In every case, the baby must be well supported, comfortable, safe and secure. Ultimately, you must carefully consider the advice from the manufacturers of your pushchair and decide exactly when your baby is ready to be taken over rough ground.

## Adequate clothing to keep your child warm

Minimise the fuss and faffing by choosing all-in-one garments with as few zips, laces, buckles, poppers, hook and eyes as possible. Good outdoor shops stock romper suits made in a variety of fabrics for babies, toddlers and even pre-schoolers. Some have securely attached gloves, booties and hoods that can defy the most cunning of little hands!

A simple vest and sleep suit with a fleece romper suit close at hand makes a straightforward, comfortable starting point. Carry another top layer if it is particularly cold. One-piece waterproofs are a must for children who disembark for a bit of walking every now and then, as puddles have a fascinating attraction.

## Spare clothing

We recommend a spare vest and sleep suit except on the shortest of trips, in case your baby takes you by surprise!

## Protection from the wind

A fleece-lined cosytoes with an outer shell makes a good investment for the four-season walker. If necessary, make adjustments so that it fastens right up to the top, covering your baby's torso as well as their legs.

## Protection from the rain

A well-fitting waterproof rain cover is a standard accessory for most ATPs (see Figure 2). Become practised at fitting it before you are caught out in a downpour, where speed is of the essence.

## Protection from the sun

It is vital that you are able to protect your children's skin during the summer months. Ultra-violet rays can damage delicate young skin, even when the sky is hazy.

Always dress your child in long sleeves and

**Figure 2.** A raincover offers superb protection from both wind and rain.

trousers and wearing a well-fitting peaked hat with neck protection. Pack a sun block that is suitable for children. A cloth can be draped over the hood of the pushchair to protect sleeping babies.

## Milk

Bottle-fed babies can present a bit of a challenge, particularly if they refuse all milk that is not warmed to their preferred temperature! We recommend pre-mixed cartons for the easy-going sort. If your baby prefers warm milk and the walk is short, simply prepare a warmer than usual bottle and wrap it in foil before you start. By the time your baby hollers, it should have cooled to a suitable temperature.

If you are planning a long day you will need to mix fresh milk whilst on your journey. We recommend taking the warm water in a flask and the measured milk powder in empty sterile bottles. When your baby cries, take a bottle and add water.

## Food

Babies can be fed using their favourite jar and a spoon. We recommend crisps or an apple for older children because these take the longest to eat! Also, the crisp packet acts as a kind of amusing puzzle for your toddler.

## Nappy Changing

Take two nappies with some wipes and before long you'll be so practised that you will think nothing of doubling up your 'top of the range' Gore-Tex as a makeshift changing mat.

## Puncture repairs

Checking that your pushchair is roadworthy before leaving home can save a lot of backache. Be prepared for the fact that punctures *will* happen – especially if there are thorns or brambles on the path. ATP tyres can be filled with "Green Slime" to protect them from the effect of puncturing. The theory is that the liquid is forced through the puncture and seals the hole but in our experience it neither prevents punctures, nor lessens their effect. We therefor recommend that you carry a puncture repair kit and suitable pump that you have had practice using.

To reduce problems with punctures, also consider thorn-resistant inner tubes or an anti-puncture lining between tube and tyre – Kevlar® linings are the most effective, but the most expensive

## Simple first-aid kit

The contents of your first-aid kit will be a personal choice, depending on how far from civilisation you will be straying and which lotions and potions you prefer to use for your children. You may wish to consider a bivvy bag or foil blanket, a whistle and a torch, plasters to soothe blisters, insect repellent and an infant Paracetamol. It is wise to carry a mobile telephone during a long walk. (Dial 999 for mountain rescue and be prepared to give the casualty's age, a description of the injury, your location and the grid reference of where you left your car, as detailed at the start of each route description.) It should however be noted that mobile phones do not have complete, uninterrupted reception throughout the Lake District as the hills tend to get in the way!

## Your own equipment

It is surprising how easy it can be to forget this! Include protective clothing, food and drink for everyone else who is walking.

## A more serious note

Thousands of families enjoy the British countryside every year without mishap. However, these routes are not just walks-in-the-park although extra precautions can be taken to ensure they are just as safe. The higher fells can be extremely exposed and weather forecasts are not always reliable. Preventing these known problems is better than having to deal with them when they occur. If the correct equipment and clothing are used for your children and yourselves it is highly unlikely that any exposure problems will occur. It is, however, sensible to be aware of potential medical conditions that result from over-exposure to the elements.

## Hypothermia

Lakeland weather can change dramatically during the course of a day and you should always be prepared for the worst. Babies and small children are particularly vulnerable to hypothermia (being too cold) because they have a large surface area compared to their volume. As an added complication, it is very hard to judge the temperature of a sedentary baby who is strapped into a pushchair, especially whilst you are exercising vigorously and generating heat. Be particularly vigilant on windy days as these can be very chilly, even if the sun is shining.

It is certainly possible to enjoy walking in the winter months – but be careful. Keep an eye on the colour of your baby's skin and be alerted if it is abnormally pale. Check your baby's temperature by feeling their chest or back with your fingers. Ensure that your own hand is not cold so that you get a proper estimate. Monitor your child's mood and watch out for them becoming quiet or withdrawn. An enjoyable walk can become an emergency if a baby is just a little too cool for a little too long, and mild hypothermia will become severe unless the core body temperature is raised.

If you suspect that your child is too cold, first make sure that they are thoroughly protected from both wind and rain. Remove any clothing that may have become wet. Add further layers of clothing and a hat or a hood if you have not already done so. A foil blanket or plastic bivvy bag can be wrapped around your child to prevent further cooling. Give chocolate to toddlers and older children; their bodies will quickly absorb this and use it to increase their core temperature.

Older children who are cold will warm up if they are allowed to walk alongside the pushchair, but measure this up carefully against returning to the car as quickly as possible.

If your young baby is very cold, put him or her inside your clothes and as close to your skin as possible. Go home and get them checked by a medical professional.

Hyperthermia: bear in mind that it is also possible for a baby to overheat. Babies cannot produce sweat in order to lose heat by evaporation and an overdressed, swaddled baby can easily become hyperthermic (too warm). Conversely, a toddler may sweat so much that they lose a dangerous amount of fluid. A child who is overheating may appear to have a normal temperature when you feel their skin. However, telltale signs include a flushed, clammy or damp skin, a more rapid breathing and higher pulse rate than normal, dry nappies, thirst and nausea. Once you detect these symp-

**Figure 3.** Babies are dressed in multiple layers. Cosytoes offer additional protection for your children.

toms, make a rapid response before the situation becomes more serious. Give your child a drink, stop them from exercising, remove some clothing and ensure that they are shaded. Seriously elevated temperatures are life threatening, so take care.

Whilst all this sounds terrifying, it should be put in perspective. The hills of North Lakeland are alive with the sounds of children and your family life will be enriched by introducing your children to their natural beauty. You are responsible adults, just behave like them and take proper precautions.

For the adult, it is unlikely that more than a blister kit will be required during any of these walks. However, it may be worth considering participating in a local first-aid course. It feels great to have the confidence that you could deal competently with any incident, either at home or whilst travelling. These courses will also be able to advise on suitable first-aid equipment to carry on the walks.

# Walk 1: Allerdale Ramble

*With superb views of Derwent Water, the route follows an old miners' track along the side of Cat Bells, and is a popular walk for tourists. Using part of the Allerdale Ramble, a long distance footpath in the Lake District, the walk provides the opportunity for some reasonable exertion as there are some relatively steep up-hill stretches. The route lends itself to all season walking, with the return stretch on a very quiet road.*

**Starting Point:** From Portinscale follow sign posts to Grange. Car Park is on left, after a cattle grid. (Grid reference: 247212)

**Distance:** 2km (circular). Allow 1½ hours

**Terrain:** Old miners' track with some vigorous climbs. Suitable for all-year-round walking.

**Maps:** Ordnance Survey Explorer OL 4 or Landranger 89 or 90

1. From the car park walk back down the road over the cattle grid, ignoring the track that climbs the hillside on the right. The small hill of Swineside, covered in trees, can be seen on the left. At the junction, follow the road round sharply to the right towards Grange.

2. Continue along the road for 20m to the track on the right of the road. Follow the track uphill – fantastic views of Derwent Water will come into view on the left through the trees. The track climbs steadily, diverging from the road. The track contours along the flanks of Cat Bells on the right, the peak of which you will shortly view.

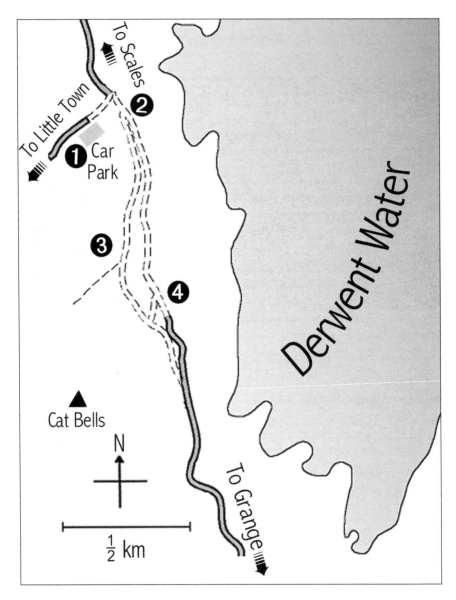

3. As the track levels out, a narrow pathway to the right leads to a rapid ascent of Cat Bells. Don't take it but proceed on to cross over the beck and enjoy the views at the highest point of the

**Figure 4.** Derwent Water from the Allerdale Ramble

walk (see Figure 4). Continue past a single, minimalist bench, which is little more than a plank of wood between two supports.

4.   Pass over the next beck as the track drops down towards the road again. After 200m take the grassy track that drops to the road behind and to the left. Return along the road back to the car park. While this is a very quiet road, care must still be taken by keeping to the right-hand edge of the road at all times.

# *Walk 2: Bassenthwaite*

*This is a pleasant walk off the beaten track, taking in calm, tranquil forests and open farmland. During the summer months the adventurous family can, in the space of a few hours, cram in all these activities – a play in the park, an energetic climb, a sedate stroll under the forest canopy, a ford crossing, an exciting descent, and duck feeding! There is even a perfectly designed ATP washer to remove the odd bit of mud at the end of the walk. Interested? Then read on!*

**Starting Point:** Bassenthwaite village lies 2km due east from the northerly tip of Bassenthwaite. Approaching Bassenthwaite from Keswick on the A591, Bassenthwaite village has a small lane forming a ring around it. Driving in a clockwise direction on this lane look out for the children's play area next to a stream. Park your car here. (Grid reference: 230323)

**Distance:** 4km (circular). Allow 2½ hours

**Terrain:** Bridleways. Some short steep ascents & descents. Can be very muddy in winter. Some ATP carrying is required. The ford crossing confines this walk to the exclusive use of Wellington Boots.

**Maps:** Ordnance Survey Explorer OL 4 or Landranger 89 or 90

---

1. Starting in the play area by the swings, follow Halls Beck upstream to the small bridge by the Sun Inn pub. Cross over the bridge, turn left and then, almost immediately, turn right up the hill. Pass Hill Farm (on the left) and follow the bridleway sign posted on the right.

2. Follow the track to a wooden gate and enter an open field, keeping the edge of the forest on the left. Look for a slight gap in the

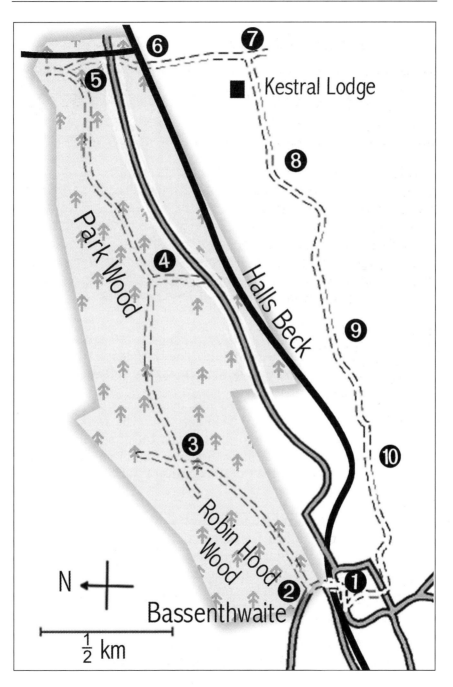

N ←+

$\frac{1}{2}$ km

**Figure 5.** At the top of the climb into the forest – an easy, flat track.

forest, (up to the left), after 100m. Climb toward this gap; a faint track can just about be made out. The track leads to a gate into the forest. Having arrived at the gate take a well-earned rest.

3.  The next short section is steep and, depending on the condition of the path, the ATP may need carrying. The walkers will be consoled to know this will be the last bit of serious exertion required on the walk! Follow the track for 200m, climbing to a much more suitable track in the depths of the forest. Turn right along this track.

4.  Cherish the opportunity for a stroll on a pleasant forest track (see Figure 5). Follow for 0.5km until the track bends to the right. Views of Skiddaw can be seen (on a good day) by looking down the track to the road. Do not continue down the track; rather, take the left track continuing up into the forest.

5.  This section will offer shade under even the fiercest sun. Follow the track for 0.5km, climbing steadily, until the upper edge of forest is reached. The track leads to a gate that, at the time of

writing, had a sign warning of a bull in the field. Don't worry, the route does not go in this direction! Take a sharp right down the hill by the way-marked wooden posts with horseshoes on. A short but fairly steep descent, following the stream to the left, ends at the road. For those less sure-footed, it may be worth two people holding onto the ATP during the descent or, alternatively, have one adult walking in front of the ATP as the hill is cautiously descended.

6. Cross straight over the road (keeping an eye out for traffic) and follow the track along Halls Beck to the wooden bridge. At this point, the walkers will be glad they are wearing their Wellington boots. Cross over the ford or, alternatively, carry the children and ATP separately across the narrow bridge. After the ford, go left for 20m to a post marking a bridleway to the right. Follow the posts up this very short steep section to a gate and style. Views of Skiddaw, Blencathra and Whitewater Dash waterfalls can be seen from here.

7. At the gate, turn left and follow the faint path, keeping a fence on the left. Drop down into small beck and out the other side. Continue in the same direction until Kestrel Lodge can be seen on the left. Walk towards the two gates directly in front of the lodge, taking the smaller gate on the right. An awkward plank runs along the bottom of this gate, possibly requiring some lifting of the ATP to cross. Through the gate, take a right, downhill, past the side of Kestrel Lodge. At the end of the fence, continue in the same direction by the dry stone wall. A third of the way along the drystone wall, on the right, there is a style and gate. Go through the gate.

8. Head towards a metal gate at the left-hand corner of the opposite side of field. A white wooden post to the right of the gate will come into view, pointing to the next gate to pass through

9. Follow the fence down to the next gate that is now visible. Continue through to the beck and then through the next gate. Continue in same direction keeping to the centre of the next

field. Two metal gates will appear on the far wall. 100m to the right of these is another white post marking the route. Head for this post. The gate here has disintegrated and consisted, at the time of writing, of two separate gates lashed to posts. Pass through these.

10. Follow stumps of previously cut down trees along the next field, passing through a metal gate. Continue along the side of a fence and then a hedgerow towards the village of Bassenthwaite. At the edge of this field are two gates, one blue and one rusty brown. Go through the rusty brown gate following the track back to the village green. Take a right, past the post box, down Cooper Dub, past cottages and back to the playground and your parked car.

Take the opportunity of giving the ATP a dip in the beck using the paving stones set near the water level – but be careful not to let go of the ATP!

# *Walk 3: Bowness Knot*

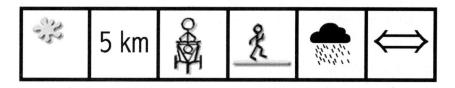

*On the northern shore of Ennerdale Water, this walk follows the lakeside to the east, reaching Char Dub, the main river that feeds the lake. The route offers some superb views of this less frequented part of the northern lakes. Ideal for all-year-round walking, the hard-packed access track is not often used by motor vehicles.*

**Starting Point:** Bowness Knot car park on north-east shore of Ennerdale Water (Grid reference: 110154)

**Distance:** 5km (there and back). Allow 2 hours

**Terrain:** Wide hardpack road. Flat.

**Maps:** Ordnance Survey Explorer OL 4 or Landranger 89

---

1. From the car park re-join the road and continue in same direction, on foot, walking down towards the lakeside. Spectacular views of Crag Fell, Revelin Crag, and Anglers Crag can be seen across the lake. The track is ideal for ATPs, being hard and firm throughout the walk, providing good all-year-round access to this splendid lake.

2. Pass a small outcrop of land covered in trees. While the approach gives it the appearance of an island, a thin finger of land joins it with the main land. This offers a pleasant place for an early snack or a picnic using the park benches.

3. There are no restrictions to the water's edge, allowing the opportunity for children to paddle in the lake. It is shallow at the edges

**Figure 6.** Ennerdale Water from the forest track.

and slopes gently, making it ideal for young children. The road is only used by Forestry Commission traffic and Youth Hostel residents and is very quiet. Cross over bridge at Smithy Beck.

4.  Continuing on the track, the eastern-most part of the lake is reached. The track then continues along Char Dub, the river that feeds the lake. The river has pleasant pebble banks. This again provides an opportunity for children to paddle, this time in moving water.

5.  500m further down the track a space age looking bridge is reached. This is the limit of the walk and ATPers can turn back and retrace their footsteps back to the car park.

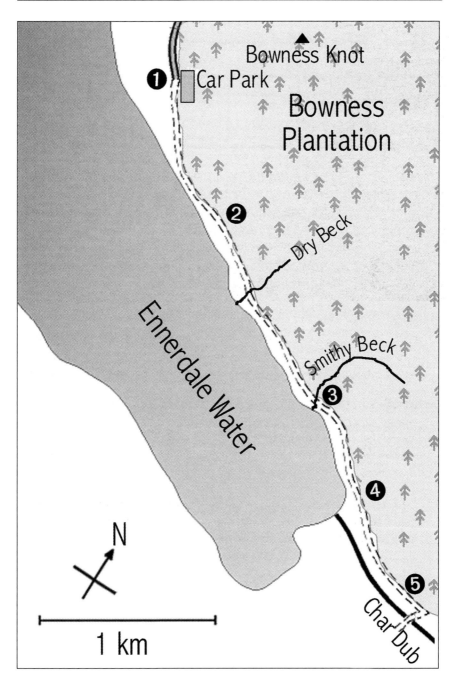

Bowness Knot

Car Park

Bowness
Plantation

Dry Beck

Smithy Beck

Ennerdale Water

Char Dub

N

1 km

# Walk 4: Bowscale Tarn

*Bowscale Tarn is a beautiful, remote tarn hidden in the hillside above Bowscale Village. It is accessed via excellent terrain and is an ideal spot for playing and picnicking. The journey to the tarn provides excellent views across the valley to the ridge beyond. The thorn in this bed of roses is the gradient; this walk involves about an hour of very strenuous uphill pushing and should not be undertaken lightly.*

**Starting Point:** From the A66 take the road signposted to Mungrisdale. Bowscale is situated 2km north of Mungrisdale. Park in the lay-by on the right-hand side, just before the road bends very sharply right past some houses. A brown wooden signpost in the lay-by reads "Dalemain Estate, Bowscale Moss". (Grid reference: 359316)

**Distance:** 4km (there and back). Allow 3 hours

**Terrain:** Excellent mix of concrete, gravel and grass. Suitable for wet and dry days.

**Maps:** Ordnance Survey Explorer OL 5 or Landranger 90

1.  Walk along the tarmac road towards the stone buildings. Take the bridleway on the left, just as the road begins to bend sharply right through the houses. Pass open grassland that rises on the left and go past a couple of houses to the right, including a red and white house with a double garage.

2.  Pass through the gate marked "Dalemain Estate" and walk alongside a stone wall to the right. The path rises slightly and it quickly assumes an open, exposed feel as the village is left

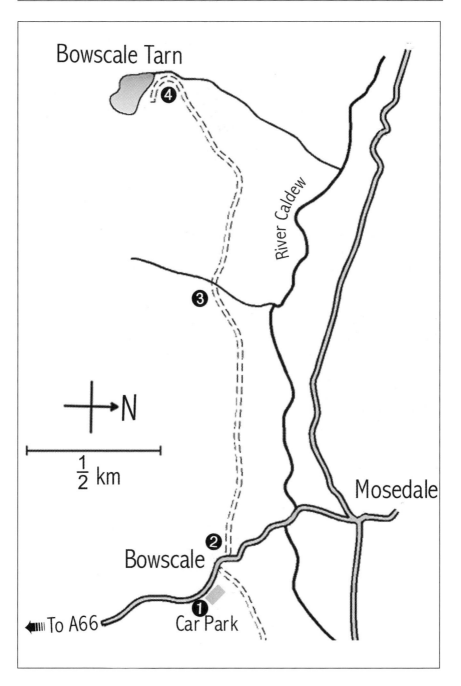

behind. Enjoy excellent views of the valley and the ridge beyond before passing through another gate and over a tiny stream. The track can be seen climbing steeply as it slices through the hillside ahead.

**Figure 7.** Bowscale Tarn and surrounding crags

3.  The path becomes so steep that it begins to undercut the bank on the left. It crosses a stream full of rushes and continues in the same vein, passing over three further streams. The stony track under-foot gives way to well-drained grass as the landscape to the left forms a bowl shape. The footpath approaches the shoulder of the hill, which drops away sharply to the right.

4.  As the path draws nearer to the tarn it becomes yet steeper and winds to the left over rocky grass. This section will be particu-larly cold and exposed if the weather is poor. The path is met by a noisy stream before levelling out to reveal the tarn, nestled in an impressive craggy amphitheatre. It is an ideal location to rest before retracing the route (see Figure 7).

# *Walk 5: Burnbanks*

*Situated on the north eastern tip of Haweswater reservoir, the walk begins on the valley floor below the dam which keeps a 30m wall of water in place! Climbing to the edge of the reservoir on its western shore, a superb track, that is ideally suited for ATPs shows the way. Take in the views of this fantastic reservoir and marvel at the concrete dam that was completed in 1955. With no navigational challenges, enjoy this splendid part of the Lake District, which, apart from the initial climb to the top of the dam, offers an easy, exertion-free ATP route.*

**Starting Point:** Burnbanks parking area. Look for a track signposted "MCWW Footpath fell-side track via north-west shore of Haweswater to Upper Martindale". (Grid reference: 508161)

**Distance:** 4km (there and back). Allow 2½ hours

**Terrain:** Good wide bridleway tracks (impossible to get lost!). Short initial climb, then relatively flat track. Track may be wet in winter and there are several fords to cross.

**Maps:** Ordnance Survey Explorer OL 5 or Landranger 90

1. Follow the fell-side signpost up the track, past the back of the houses as it winds gently up the hill into pleasant woodland that offers shade during the summer months. The track then levels out before a hair-pin bend to the right. Continue to walk up the hill, the path ends at the edge of the forest by a style and gate.

2. Through the gate, take the left track, skirting along the top of the forest. Haweswater dam will soon come into view. It is hard to

believe that, in the past, a pleasant valley lay beneath this reservoir. It is fabled that a church in the valley that was abandoned, before the area was flooded, has a bell that can still be heard tolling from the depths when the water is choppy!

3. Pass by the dam and follow the path downhill towards the lakeside, crossing over a small ford. Fences prevent access to the lakeside in an attempt to protect the cleanliness of the water which, after a 100-mile journey underground, provides water for the Manchester area.

4. Follow the lakeside for another 400m before crossing over a wide ford.

5. After another 300m cross over another

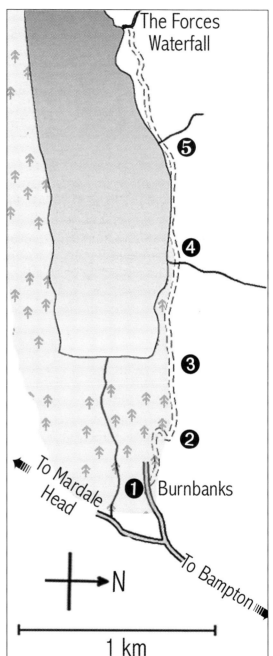

**Figure 8.** Haweswater Reservoir

ford coming from Mile Crags. This is a suitable point to turn around and retrace the route back to the start. The adventurous can continue for another 0.5km to "The Forces" waterfalls. The track does narrow down to a path and will require some ATP carrying where rock fall has obstructed the route. It is questionable whether this effort is justified – the waterfall itself being obscured for the most part by trees.

# Walk 6: Coledale

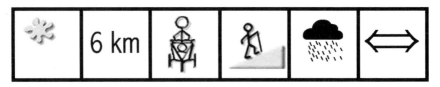

*A wonderful valley walk – experience a true sense of
remoteness without the usual climbs associated with such
escapes from the trappings of civilisation. Following the old
miners' track, the route takes you alongside Coledale Beck to
Force Crag mines. The track is firm and not too steep, making
this a suitable route for ATP first-timers.*

**Starting Point:** From Braithwaite take the road towards Whinlatter Pass.
The road turns sharply to the left and, after 200m, the car park entrance
can be seen on the left. The route begins at the left-hand side of the car
park by the start of the wide track. (Grid reference: 227237)

**Distance:** 6km (there and back). Allow 3 hours

**Terrain:** Wide tracks with gentle climbs. Suitable for all-year-round walking.

**Maps:** Ordnance Survey Explorer OL 4 or Landranger 89 or 90

1.  Follow the track that leads out onto the fell side, climbing
    gently. Good views can be seen right from the beginning of the
    walk as the car park is at 100m above sea level. As the track
    slowly bends around to the right, views of Sail and Causey Pike
    can be seen.

2.  Pass through the wooden gate and continue along the track.
    Coledale Beck can be heard down in the valley below, before it
    comes into view. The track maintains a gentle gradient as it
    continues up the valley. The height difference between the beck
    and the track reduces as the beck climbs at a faster rate than the

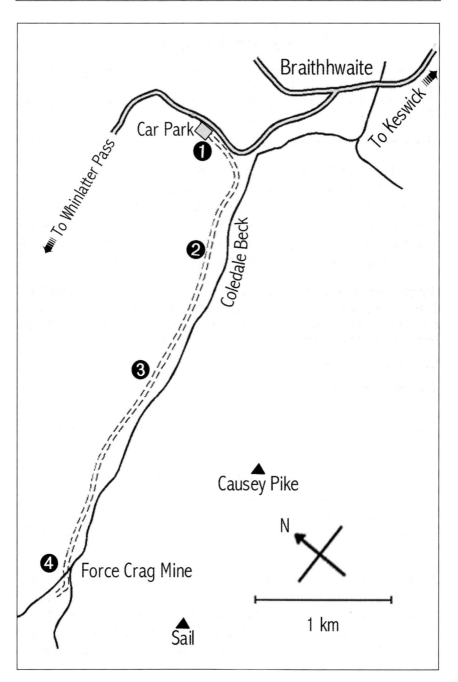

**Figure 9.** Coledale Beck and Force Crag Mine in the distance

track. The steep bracken slopes of Grisedale Pike meet the track on the right.

3.  After 1.5km from the beginning of the walk, the track slowly and almost imperceptibly bends around to the right. A disused mine comes into view with the imposing backdrop of Force Crags.

4.  The path continues to gently climb for the next 1km to the head of the valley and the stream by Force Crag mine. The route ends here as the track can be seen climbing steeply up towards Cole-dale Hause – the saddle between Hopegill Head on the right and Crag Hill on the left.

# Walk 7: Crummock Water

*This is a short walk offering intermittent views of Crummock Water through the forest edge. A good introductory walk for ATPs, the route is relatively flat and presents no great navigational challenges. The walk may also be lengthened by exploring the equally suitable path on the north-western tip of Crummock Water.*

**Starting Point:** Langthwaite Wood, National Trust Pay-and-display car park. (Grid reference: 149215)

**Distance:** 2km (there and back). Allow 1 hour.

**Terrain:** Wide forest tracks.

**Maps:** Ordnance Survey Explorer OL 4 or Landranger 89

1. From the car park go through the gate into the forest. Follow the river as it winds its way through the forest on the right.

2. At the fork, take the right-hand track that drops downwards. Continue along the track, ignoring the sharp turnoff up the hill to the left.

3. At the fork take the right-hand track.

4. At the next fork take the left track that is obstructed, in part, by a low metal bar. The right track drops towards a weir that can be heard before it is seen.

5. Climb up the track, passing by the memorial park bench, which levels out approximately 10m above the lakeside (see Figure 10).

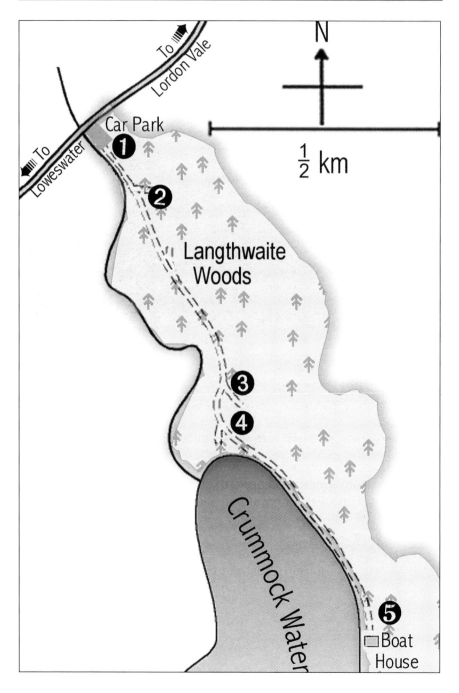

**Figure 10.** The track running along the forest edge with Crummock Water on the right.

Continue along the track until a boathouse with a tiny secluded bay at its base appears. This is the end-point of the walk. If this is not enough, the walk can be extended on the homeward journey by taking the left footpath going towards the weir (leg 4) as this follows the lake side on the western shore on an equally suitable track.

# Walk 8: The Cumbria Way

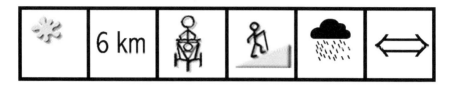

*The Cumbria Way is a long distance path (112km) travelling through the heart of the Lake District joining Ulverston in the south to Carlisle in the North. This walk follows the Cumbria Way in reverse as it winds its way from the plains and foothills of northern Cumbria towards the first group of mountains in the North Lakes, including Skiddaw and Blencathra. An ideal introductory walk for those new to ATPs; this walk offers excellent terrain, gentle slopes, and picturesque fords in this unfrequented part of the lakes (see Figure 11).*

**Starting Point:** From the A66 travelling from Penrith towards Keswick, take the road to the right signposted Mungrisdale. Follow this road for 4km, passing through Mungrisdale to Mosedale. Just after the bridge crossing the River Caldew, take a left turn by a telephone box. Follow this lane for 3km, crossing a small bridge at the end and bearing left where the lane ends. Cars may be parked either side of the track. (Grid reference: 327327)

**Distance:** 6km (there and back – can be shortened to suit) Allow 3 hours.

**Terrain:** Wide, firm bridleway, with a gentle slope.

**Maps:** Ordnance Survey Explorer OL 5 or Landranger 90

1.  Start along the track heading in a westerly direction, climbing gently.

2.  Pass a track to the left with metal gate leading to a ford. (Suitable for washing an ATP off after a muddy week of walking!)

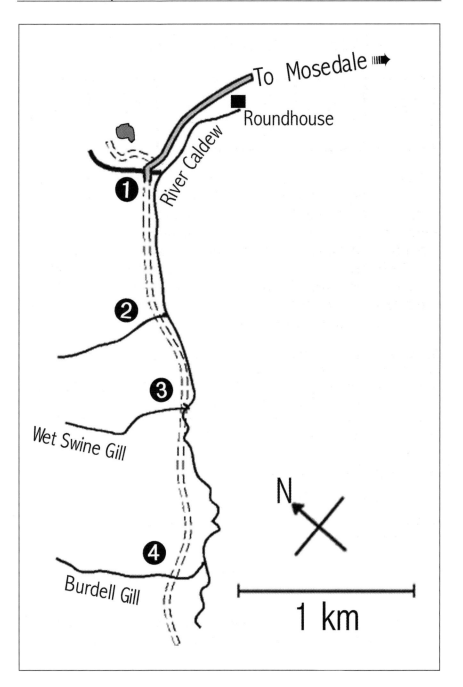

To Mosedale ⇒

■ Roundhouse

River Caldew

❶

❷

❸

Wet Swine Gill

N

❹

Burdell Gill

1 km

Figure 11. A ford crossing the Cumbria Way

3.  Follow the path to Wet Swine Gill that is easily crossed via a ford.

4.  Continue along the track for about 0.7km to the waterfalls of Burdell Gill (on the right). Cross over via the ford. At this point, the peaks of Little Man and Skiddaw can be seen directly in front, with the Skiddaw House youth hostel at the bottom of the slopes. To the left, views of Blencathra may be seen. A short distance later the terrain opens out into a flatter expanse of land where the River Caldew is split by a tiny island – an ideal place to stop and enjoy a picnic (weather permitting!)

    After a well-earned rest, enjoy the walk back to the car – all downhill!

# *Walk 9: Dalemain Country Manor*

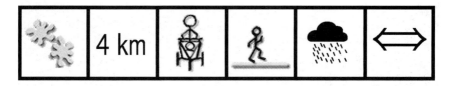

*Starting in Dacre, a small Lakeland village, this walk takes in some wonderful countryside and contains examples of splendid local architecture, including Dalemain – the family home of the Hasell family since 1679. Now open to visitors, the beautiful gardens are matched by an interior boasting rooms decorated in various period styles, including Georgian and Tudor. Snacks and refreshments are available here. A baby-carrier may be more suited to exploring Dalemain, and the owners would appreciate you parking the muddy ATP outside!*

**Starting Point:** Dacre, situated 2km north-west of Pooley Bridge. Park opposite the Horse and Farrier pub. (Grid reference: 459266)

**Distance:** 4km (there and back). Allow 2 hours.

**Terrain:** Flat tracks and Bridleways

**Maps:** Ordnance Survey Explorer OL 5 or Landranger 90

1.  The Horse and Farrier pub is on the left-hand side of the road when leaving Dacre in a northerly direction. From the pub, drop down the road into Dacre, passing a lane on the left. A red telephone box can be just seen in the corner of a building and wall covered in ivy. Turn left after the telephone box and cross over a cattle grid.

2.  At the next junction, take the left towards Dacre Castle, a property resplendent with towers and castellations. Continue along the track over a beck, the track bears round to the left into an open field. Pass through a metal gate into another field with a

**Figure 12.** The front of Dalemain

track running along its left-hand side. This track is rutted and may be wet in the winter months or after a period of rain.

3.  Walk through the gate, staying on left-hand side of the field, to the next wooden gate, past a barn and a track to the left that leads to Park House Farm. Regimented trees, planted in a neat row, line the edge of the field and stretch into the distance.

4.  Continue along the track for another 0.5km to reach a very pleasant cobbled square, with stables and a cottage, leading to the entrance to Dalemain House (see Figure 12). Drinks and snacks are available here. After a suitable rest and refreshments, return to Dacre via the track.

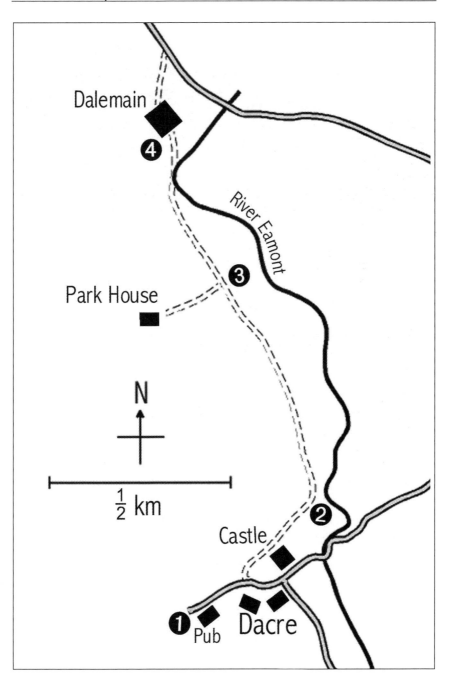

# *Walk 10: Dockray*

*Named after the nearest village, this walk lies 1km due west of Dockray on the edge of Matterdale Common. Following the coast-to-coast cycle route, the walk tracks across exposed, rolling fells and fords wide streams. The car park is situated at 408 metres above sea level and is accessed via a minor road that is likely to become icy during the winter months. For the summer months, the walk offers a good introduction to ATPing.*

**Starting Point:** On reaching Dockray, turn left at the Royal Hotel. Drive up the narrow hill to the T-junction and park in the large grassy area directly opposite. (Grid reference:380219)

**Distance:** 7km (there and back). Allow 3½ hours or shorten to suit.

**Terrain:** Smooth grass and gravelled track, some gentle climbing and wide, level plains.

**Maps:** OS Ordnance Survey Explorer OL 5 or Landranger 90

---

1.  A three-way sign post in the parking area marks Matterdale Common as the start of the walk. Pass through the gate onto the common and follow the smooth track that is formed from a mixture of grass and gravel. Walk past coniferous forest to the right and open grassland to the left.

2.  Leave the forest behind and climb the gentle hill. The path leads to Grove Beck, a small waterfall and a wide, shallow stream that requires fording (see Figure 13). A wooden bridge provides an alternative crossing for very narrow pushchairs.

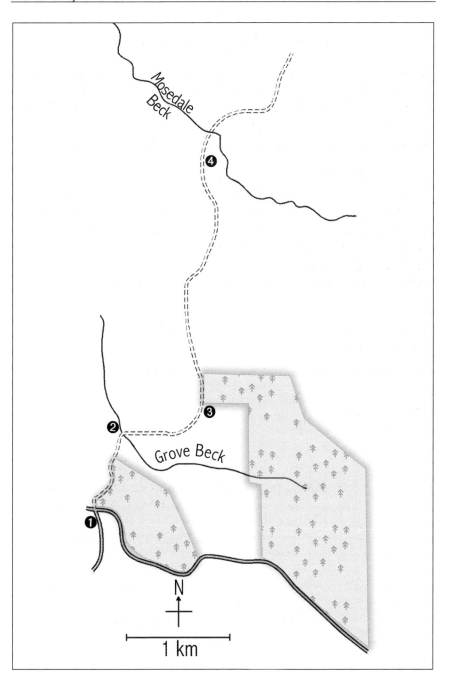

**Figure 13.** The wide shallow ford at Grove Beck

3.   The path bends to the right and levels out. Pass straight on at the
     minor fork and across the flat, comfortable terrain. The track
     continues in much the same vein, remaining very obvious and
     easy to discern. It passes Great Mel Fell to the right and Wolf
     Crags to the left. The track bears round to the left around a shoul-
     der of land coming from the flanks of Great Dodd, before passing
     a short stretch of forest on the right.

4.   Continue along the track for another 2km to Mosedale Beck.
     This is a scenic location for a break and an ideal point to turn
     back.

# Walk 11: Dodd Wood

*Dodd Wood boasts breathtaking views, terrain that was made for pushchairs and a steep, exciting downhill finale. However, what comes down must first go up! You have been warned. For the first 45 minutes of this walk, it's "heads down" for some very strenuous climbing.*

**Starting Point:** Park in The Old Sawmill Car Park. This pay-and-display car park contains public toilets and a seasonal café. (Grid reference: 235282)

**Distance:** 5km. Allow 3 hours

**Terrain:** Mixed, easy terrain including tarmac and gravel. Steep ascents and descents.

**Maps:** Ordnance Survey OL 4 and Landranger 89 or 90

1. Begin by taking the small track near the display board at the back of the car park. Cross over Skill Beck and turn left towards the road.

2. The next short, steep section of path appears to lead directly to the road, which can be seen through the sparse trees in the winter but may be shielded by vegetation during the summer. However, a junction allows for a right turn away from the road and onto the beginning of a long, steep, upward section with concrete underfoot.

3. Enjoy a steep, strenuous climb for 20 minutes, keeping the stream and valley to the right. Ignore any tracks turning off to the left or right. The path becomes marginally easier but still

extremely tiring for a further 25 minutes as the right-hand stream rises higher and becomes visible through the trees.

4.  Pass a grassy lay-by and a track on the left as the route bends around to the right. The terrain changes from solid tarmac to older, broken concrete and becomes stony as the hill begins to peak. The forest on the left gives way to scrub land and scree as the route passes over the flanks of Skiddaw.

**Figure 14.** The trees offer protection from the sun

5.  Pass another track to the left, finally reaching a wide, flat, gravelled area that presents three options; a left-hand track, a second track signed "Dodd Summit" and a hairpin track to the right. Take the left-hand route to be rewarded with excellent views of Keswick, Ullswater and Borrowdale from an impressive height.

6.  Follow the path as it sweeps round to the right, gently dropping around Scalebeck Gill. It passes a grassy lay-by on the left before contouring right to reveal spectacular views of Grisedale Pike and Bassenthwaite Lake.

7.  Continue to follow the path as it bends sharply right, ignoring both the hairpin turn on the left and the steep right option near the bend.

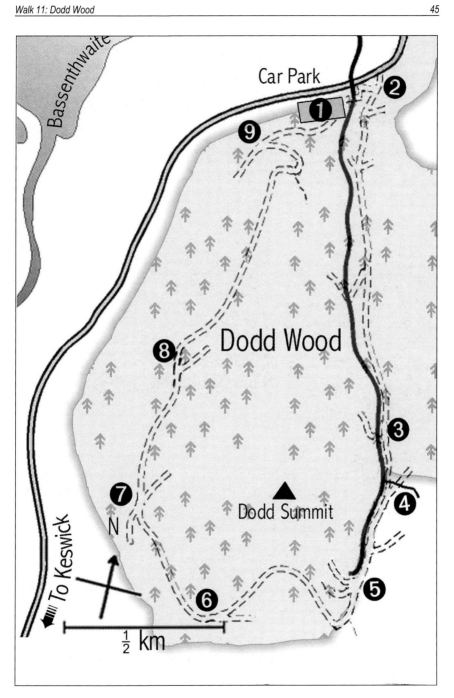

**8.** Pass a turn-off to the right. Continue along the track until it starts to weave sharply left and right over a very short distance.

**9.** A sign post is reached that reads "Keswick" to the left and "Mirehouse & Tea-rooms" to the right. An adjacent information board displays text about a current osprey project. Turn right and take care as the path winds a steep, downhill trail alongside a stream and back to the car park.

# Walk 12: Ennerdale Water

*One of the most eastern lakes in the Lake District, Ennerdale Water is about a 45-minute drive from Keswick. The walk is located on the westerly tip of the lake. Likely to be muddy in winter, the walk passes along the lakeside, through forests and returns along a short stretch of quiet road.*

**Starting Point:** Broadmoor Forest Car Park. From direction of Ennerdale Bridge, follow signs for Ennerdale Water. Pass a wooden sign post (pointing to the to scout camp), cross over a bridge and into a fenced car park on the left-hand side of road. (Grid reference: 085153)

**Distance:** 2km (circular). Allow 1½ hours

**Terrain:** A mixture of wide, flat and narrow footpaths. May be muddy in winter.

**Maps:** Ordnance Survey Explorer OL 4 or Landranger 89

1. Take the footpath at end of car park towards the lake, go through the large gate, suitably sized to accommodate ATPs. As the path joins a wide, firm track, follow to the left towards the lake.

2. The track reaches a weir at the tip of Ennerdale Water. Cross over the weir by the bridge. Pass through the wooden gate where the path becomes a little wet and muddy during the winter months. Splendid views of Ennerdale water and the surrounding mountains can be seen from here (see Figure 15). Pass some scout camp huts just inside the forest on the left.

3. Pass the corner of the forest that forms a sharp point at the side of

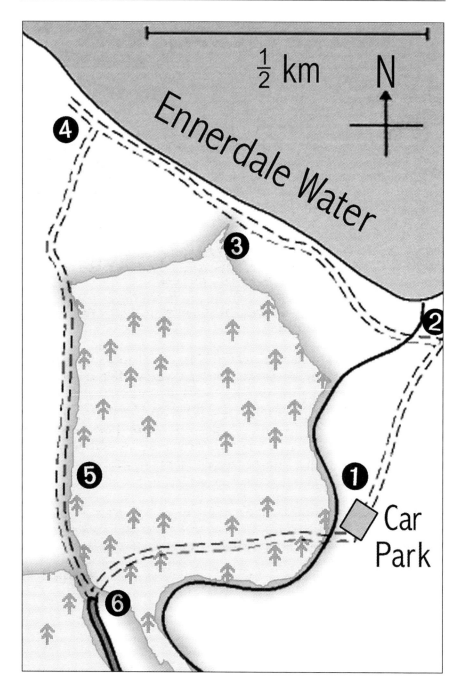

**Figure 15.** Ennerdale Water from the track.

the path. Continue through a wooden gate, following the track along edge of the lake.

4. Cross over the beck by a small metal gate. Before the gate, turn left up a narrow grassy footpath with reeds that signal wet, damp ground, most suitable for boots or wellies. Follow the track until a fence on the left appears. Be careful to avoid brushing the children's faces with the prickly bushes that you pass. Ignore the wooden gate on the right and continue along a track bordered by the forest and a dry stone wall. The track begins to improve at this point.

5. Follow the track until a large millstone is reached – its purpose is to block the track to motorised vehicles. Pass a parking area and through a wooden gate, continuing to the roadside.

6. Take a left along this quiet road leading back to the carpark.

# Walk 13: Fellside

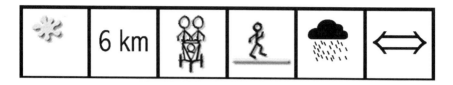

*Situated on the northern tip of the National Park, away from the tourist circuit, this walk promises the beauty of the Cumbrian fells, and solitude – an increasingly rare combination of adjectives concerning the Lake District! A track made for ATPs – the route penetrates into the group of hills that culminate in the peaks of Skiddaw and Blencathra. Following an old miner's track, crossing fords, and bridging rivers, the route ends at a disused mine with the backdrop of spectacular crags and cascading waterfalls. The mine, dating back to the 16$^{th}$ century, is still rich with minerals, including lead, copper and silver. But before you think of early retirement through prospecting – a permit is required!*

**Starting Point:** Fellside can be approached either via the A591 north of Keswick (through Uldale) or via the A66 (through Mungrisdale). Car parking spaces are available just before the gate leading to the start of the miner's track. (Grid reference: 375305)

**Distance:** 6km (there and back). Allow 3 hours.

**Terrain:** Excellent track, suitable for all-year-round walking

**Maps:** Ordnance Survey OL 4 or Landranger 90

1. Go through the metal gate at start of track and turn right. Signs on the gate give a clue to the historical significance of this track – the area is still home to a rich variety of minerals that require a permit to mine.

2. Following the track as it bends to the left into the valley, Great

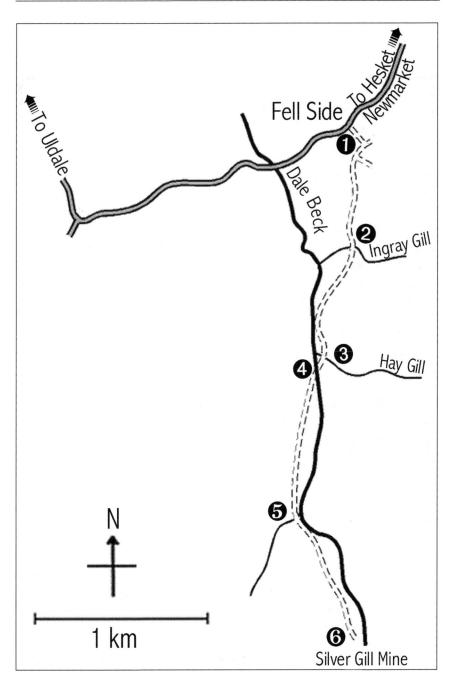

**Figure 16.** Dale Beck, looking northward

Lingy Hill can be seen in the distance. Twist around Ingray Gill, crossing over the stream before passing a single electricity pole (apparently not doing much!).

3.  Pass the remains of mine buildings on the right before crossing over the next stream at Hay Gill, next to the sheepfold.

4.  The track drops down to the valley floor (see Figure 16) and crosses Dale Beck via a bridge. Do not attempt to cross via the ford as it is quite deep! The push chair will need to be carried down the steps at the other side of the bridge.

5.  After about 0.7km, another small stream taking water from Wet Smale and Swinburn Gills is crossed.

6.  After another 0.5km along the flat track, the mine workings at the base of Roughgill and Silvergill are reached. An appreciation of the scale of the mine can be gleaned – in their heyday during the 1840s, the mines gave a yearly output of 500 tons of lead and 25 tons of copper. After a suitable rest, the return journey can also be enjoyed as it offers the alternative views of the flatter farmland plains leading towards Carlisle.

# *Walk 14: Glenderamackin*

*This route has been included for those intrepid explorers who are out to test their ATP to the limit! It includes long, steep, rocky wet sections that only the determined should attempt during the drier months. Those who dare will eventually enjoy a flat, grassy, riverside footpath and an easy ford crossing.*

**Starting point:** From the A66, follow the signposts to Mungrisdale. A lay-by for car parking is on the right just before the sharp left-hand bend into Mungrisdale. (Grid reference: 364302)

**Distance:** 4km (there and back). Allow 2½ hours

**Terrain:** Challenging short and narrow rocky sections that require some ATP carrying. Otherwise, grassy tracks and gravelled path.

**Maps:** Ordnance Survey Explorer OL 4 or Landranger 90

---

1.  After parking on the roadside, follow the road further into Mungrisdale. It bends sharply to the left and passes a road junction. The road then bends to the right where a track to the left is reached. Take this track (before the road bends to the right again).

2.  Follow the track past the white house and through the gate. The path crosses a very small stream and continues across excellent terrain. This path is visible well into the distance and can be seen ascending very steeply. Do not worry because your route soon turns off to the left and contours around Tongue Hill!

3.  The next stream must be forded because the footbridge is too narrow for a pushchair. Walk past the tributary that feeds the

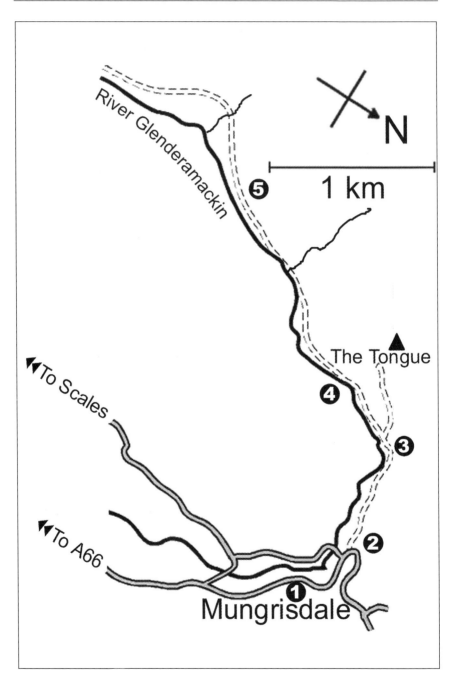

**Figure 17.** Crossing a ford leading into the River Glenderamackin

stream from the right. Take the minor left-hand footpath twenty metres further on and contour around the hill at a lower level than the main footpath.

4.  The path becomes overgrown, boggy, narrow and rocky and the pushchair must, occasionally, be lifted. The route continues to be challenging with intermittent, easier grassy sections for the next twenty minutes.

5.  Ford the next stream, marked by a small waterfall, while enjoying views of Bannerdale Crags to the right. Continue up the hill onto drier, grassy terrain as the river drops away to the left. This easier terrain continues in the same vein at least to the next bridge and this makes for a pleasant picnic site and landmark at which to turn back.

# Walk 15: Glenderaterra

*This walk offers an exposed mountainous feel with minimal effort. The terrain is perfect, the gradient is very kind. Small, manageable ford crossings offer great entertainment for young children. There are numerous suitable picnic sites and shallow rivers for children to play in. After heavy rain, the fords may become impassable. Nearest hot food and refreshments are in Threlkeld.*

**Starting Point:** Take the road to Blencathra Centre and follow the right, rutted track leading to the car park (the left fork leads to Blencathra Centre). The walk begins at the top end of the Blencathra Car Park. (Grid reference: 302257)

**Distance:** 4km (there and back). Allow 2 hours

**Terrain:** A bridleway track with some fords to cross. A gentle climb achieving a good sense of remoteness. A good all-year-round route.

**Maps:** Ordnance Survey Explorer OL 4 or Landranger 90

1.  The track starts with a moderate incline for three minutes (see Figure 18) before flattening out. It bears right, providing good views of Lonscale fell while contouring around the side of Blencathra on excellent terrain. Look for a river on the left, running along the bottom of the valley.

2.  The path becomes steeper as it approaches a small waterfall that can be crossed via a shallow ford. Follow the path down to the bottom of the valley, crossing a bridge at the next waterfall. The terrain becomes stony and uneven up to the bridge at the bottom

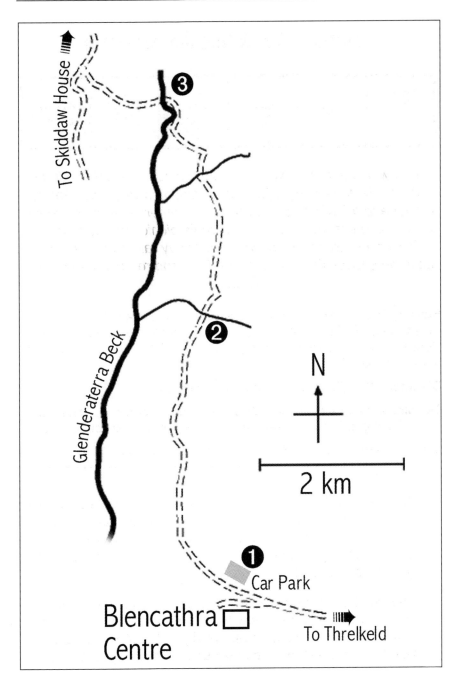

**Figure 18.** The gentle track invites the ATPer onwards

of the valley and it will be muddy if there has been recent rainfall.

3.  The bridge at the bottom of the valley provides an ideal place to turn around, although the more adventurous can continue a further 1.5km to Skiddaw House, though those who do this must negotiate a short steep section and cross a larger ford.

# Walk 16: Grisedale

*The short, sharp climb at the start of this walk is quickly forgotten on reaching a beautiful valley that has a superb aspect (see Figure 19) for enjoying views of Helvellyn to the west and Ullswater to the east. This is a good all year round walk with no navigational challenges.*

**Starting point:** Limited parking is available on the verge of the cul-de-sac alongside Patterdale Hall (leg 2). Otherwise, park in the crescent shaped lay-by in front of Patterdale Church. The church is on the right-hand side when approaching from Glenridding, opposite the Mountain Rescue building. (Grid reference: 393161)

**Distance:** 4km (there and back). Allow 2½ hours

**Terrain:** Initially, very steep concrete road. Flat gravel track and rocky footpath beyond.

**Maps:** Ordnance Survey Explorer OL 5 or Landranger 90

---

1.  Beginning at Patterdale Church, cross the road and walk alongside Ullswater towards Glenridding. Continue past the sports ground on the left-hand side. Turn left up the steep tarmac lane just before Patterdale Hall, sign posted "Helvellyn, Grisedale Tarn".

2.  Follow the lane with the stream on the right-hand side, passing by "Home Farm" (bed and breakfast) on the left.

3.  Follow the winding lane as it begins to climb steeply out of the village, passing a coniferous wood on the left. As progress is

**Figure 19.** The reward after the initial climb – Grisedale Valley.

made, the stream on the right drops lower and lower. Continue
for fifteen minutes until the road flattens out and gives way to a
wide valley that provides impressive views of the ridge up to
Helvellyn.

4. Go through the gate directly ahead rather than following the
   main track around to the right. A slate embedded subtly into the
   wall on the left with the words "Grisedale Tarn, Grasmere" indi-
   cates the correct route.

5. The terrain hereafter is ideal for All-Terrain Pushchairs and the
   route follows the high wall to the left. It remains well marked
   and obvious, winding through stocked fields and periodically
   returning to the river.

6. Continue straight through all sets of gates and past some high
   crags on the left. Upon reaching a small complex of buildings,
   the track bends sharply to the right and becomes more rutted,
   narrow and rocky. This is a suitable place to rest and return,
   retracing the route back to the car. The track however, can be
   happily negotiated a good deal further, and so the limiting factor
   to this walk is likely to be the weather or the children rather than
   to the terrain.

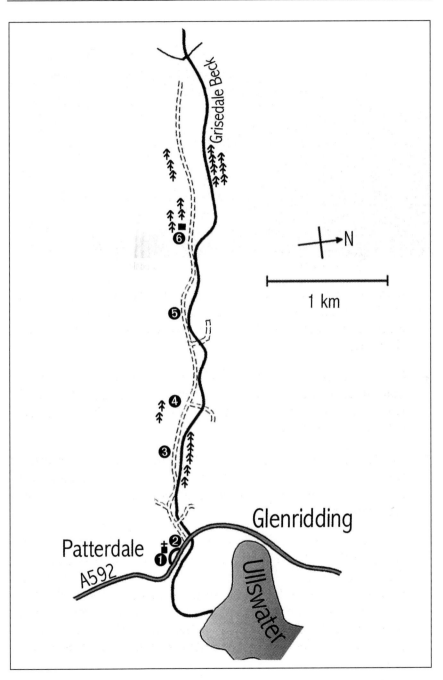

# Walk 17: Haweswater

*Situated on the southern tip of Haweswater reservoir, the walk offers some superb scenery. The route is fairly rough, and the ATP will need to be carried over larger rocks at times. With the addition of the climb, this is not for those walkers seeking a leisurely stroll! The path is also narrow in places, which makes it difficult for a double ATP. The adventurous will, however, be rewarded with the chance of witnessing the sight of a pair of golden eagles (binoculars will be required for this unless you are lucky!) Potential collectors need not bother trying to collect any eggs – the site is under 24-hour surveillance and the exact location of the eagles nest is a well guarded secret!*

**Starting Point:** Car park at southern tip of Haweswater. (Grid reference: 469107)

**Distance:** 2km (there and back). Allow 1½ hours

**Terrain:** Route will be very wet in winter. Bumpy path, narrow at times. ATP requires carrying in places. Steep climb – definitely for those who want to push the envelope of ATPing, this will challenge the fittest of walkers!

**Maps:** Ordnance Survey Explorer OL 5 or Landranger 90

1.  From the car park, follow the footpath to a signpost reading "MCWW public footpath Gatesgarth pass to Longsdale". Cross over the beck via the bridge, climb for a short section.

2.  As the path forks, take the right-hand path, sign-posted to Bampton.

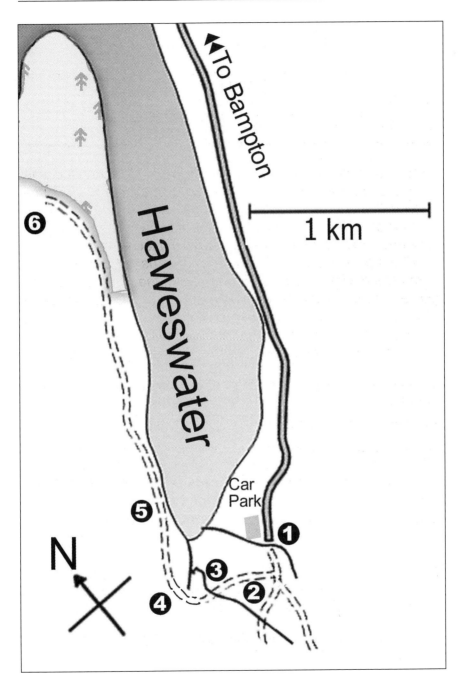

**Figure 20.** Haweswater from The Rigg

3.  Walk downhill along the bumpy track following the drystone wall on the right. This path is typical of those made by volunteer teams to protect popular routes from severe erosion. A few steps will be reached which will require carrying the ATP down. Drop to the base of the valley where splendid views of Harter fell and Mardale Ill Bell can be enjoyed. Cross over the beck by the narrow wooden bridge.

4.  Continue along bumpy track made of discrete boulders and stones crossing another beck before crossing a bridge over the main source of water into Haweswater. Turn right along the path.

5.  The path has many partially exposed drainage channels running across it, which, whilst preventing the path becoming a stream after heavy rain, do not help the ATPers in their progress up the slope! Some rockfall across the path will require the ATP to be carried for around 20m. Looking down towards the lake during the summer months, its lower level reveals some

drystone walls. These are a reminder of the farmland and villages that were sacrificed during the creation of this reservoir.

6. Pass along the coniferous plantation on "The Rigg" – a narrow peninsula jutting into the lake. The path will now progress uphill along the side of the forest (see Figure 20.). At the top of the slope is a gap in the drystone wall that is our route to the top of the slope. This marks the end of the walk and, by this stage, the ATPer will want a good rest. Take in the views of Riggindale Valley and Kidsty Pike. The skies above here are the hunting area for golden eagles – keep your eyes peeled!

# Walk 18: Heughscar Hill

*Askham is a classic, beautiful little Lakeland village situated 5km due south of Penrith, and is easily accessed from the M6 motorway. Askham is well served by a village post office and pub that serves cooked meals. Look out for the local toy shop offering unique, quality hand-crafted toys. With pleasant, wide tracks, views of Ullswater and High Street can be seen while circumnavigating Heughscar Hill.*

**Starting Point:** Askham Village. Ample car parking spaces available (Grid reference: 512238)

**Distance:** 6km (Circular Walk). Allow 2½ hours

**Terrain:** Good wide bridleway tracks (impossible to get lost!) and a short stretch along a minor road. Some moderate climbs, but worth it for the views.

**Maps:** Ordnance Survey Explorer OL 5 or Landranger 90

---

1.  Beginning in Askham, walk up the lane opposite the village post office. Passing the village green, a 'dead-end' road sign, and some wonderful oak trees, the lane climbs out of the village towards Askham Fell.

2.  Pass through the gate and over the cattle grid into the Lowther Estate.

3.  At the fork, take the right-hand track, following the drystone wall on the left. Follow the track as it becomes more rocky and grassy (see Figure 21).

**Figure 21.** Take the right-hand track up towards Heughscar Hill

4. At the next fork, take the right-hand track climbing gently towards the copse. On reaching it, go through the gate, passing the copse on the right onto open land. Head straight across to the left-hand corner of the next wood, reaching the top of the hill.

5. Take the left track just before the corner of the woods, dropping downwards. Views of Ullswater and the old Roman road (High Street) can be seen from here.

6. After 0.5km the track ends at a T-junction. Turn right along the track for a further 0.5km.

7. A heap of white stones on the left marks the next turn-off as the track starts to drop downhill. Turn right at the stones, climbing for 200m (don't worry – it doesn't last forever!). Once the track levels out, continue for 1km towards woods – Heugh Scar can be seen on the left. Stay on the main track, ignoring turn-offs to left or right.

8. The track crosses under an electricity line and approaches a

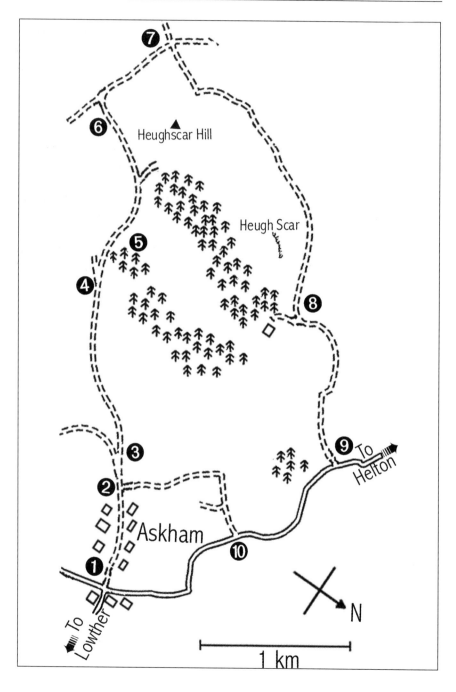

Heughscar Hill

Heugh Scar

Askham

To Helton

To Lowther

N

1 km

building. Follow the track down to the left of the building towards a wooden gate. 50m before the gate your route leaves the track by a small wooden gate in a dry-stone wall on the right – easily missed! Go straight across the field, joining a track serving as a driveway to the building on the right. Turn left along the track for 1km, and drop onto road.

9.  Crossing over the cattle grid, turn right down the road towards Askham. After 700m, take the track to the right.

10. The track gently climbs up a slope. Ignoring the turn-off to the left (signposted "private land") continue up the track for a further 300m where the track bears round to the right. After a short distance, the track joins the first road that you climbed at the beginning of the walk. Turn left along the road, back into Askham.

# Walk 19: Keswick Railway

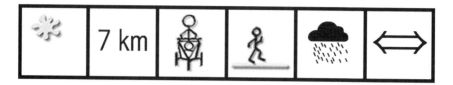

*The walk follows the route of the old Keswick railway line, along the River Greta. A straight-forward off-road stroll with easy terrain and no hills! A good choice for foul weather days – choose a suitable duration for the walk and turnaround at half-time. A steep slope plunging down towards the river is contoured by a board walk, giving this walk a little bit of extra spice. End the day in the sports centre and swimming pool or enjoy the best of the Northern Lakes outdoor gear shops and cafés.*

**Starting Point:** Keswick Bell Close car park

**Distance:** Up to 10km for Threlkeld. Allow 2½ hours for walk to Brundholme and back – 7km (Grid reference: 267234)

**Terrain:** Wide and flat bridleway, can become puddled after heavy rain.

**Maps:** Ordnance Survey Explorer OL 4 or Landranger 90

1.  Turn right out of Bell Close car-park in the centre of Keswick and look for signs to the motor museum and art gallery. Cross over at the traffic lights and walk up Station Road to the corner of Fitz Park, passing a youth hostel and a French restaurant. Cross the bridge (Bridge 1), passing the museum and art gallery on the left. Continue to the sports centre car-park

2.  Walk to the right of the sports centre, following the signs for "railway footpath". Pass the old station and turn left at the first fork. Pass under the fly-over and through a gate. There is a metal sculpture on the left, to mark the creation of the national cycle

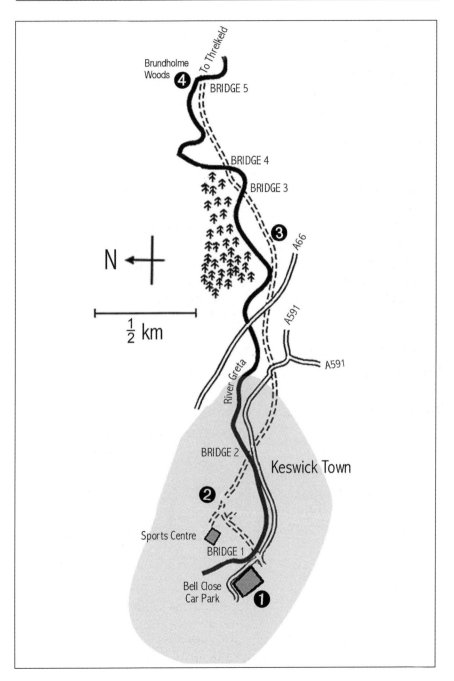

network. Continue along to a fairly long boardwalk (see Figure 22), negotiating the sides of a steep slope.

3.  Pass a caravan site, on the left, and cross a bridge (marked Bridge 3 on map). Next on the left is an information board that explains the history of the area. The River Greta and the railway served numerous bobbing mills during the 19th century. By the mid-1800s the Lake District housed over 120 bobbin mills, which supplied half of the world's demand. Fierce competition from abroad ultimately led to their demise.

4.  The railway continues with similar scenery, crossing the river three times (bridges 2, 3 and 4 on map) during the next 1km stretch. Straight after the fourth bridge (marked as Bridge 4 on map), a signpost for Brundholme Woods and a single park bench is reached. A meadow is situated alongside – suitable as a children's play and picnic area. The track continues for another 3km to Threlkeld. Pushchair walkers will, however, find Brundhome woods a suitable point to turn around and retrace the route back into Keswick along this very pretty river.

**Figure 22.** The board walk

# Walk 20: Loweswater

*An ideal walk for those wanting spectacular scenery without the usual exertion associated with such vistas. This walk is an ideal introduction to ATPing, with wide, flat tracks, some manageable fords; ATPing doesn't get much better than this!*

**Starting Point:** Maggie's Bridge near south-east tip of Loweswater. (Grid reference: 135210)

**Distance:** 4km (there and back). Allow 2 hours

**Terrain:** Wide bridleway tracks, relatively flat

**Maps:** Ordnance Survey Explorer OL 4 or Landranger 89

1. From the car park, return to the road. Pass through the gate and over Dub Beck, ignoring the track to the left.

2. Follow the pleasant track across open farmland towards Loweswater. To the left is the distinct hill of Carling Knot. Continue along the track, passing over the cattle-grid. The track is solid and is suitable for all-year-round walking. Pass over another cattle-grid as the path joins the side of the lake.

3. At Watergate farm, take the shortcut across the field, as this avoids the opening and closing of two gates around the farm premises. At the end of the field, cross over a small stream and turn right, going through the small gate into Holme Wood. A park bench is hidden behind the dry-stone wall, offering a good venue for a picnic. Fantastic views of the lake are visible on the left on a track that was made for ATPs! (see Figure 23).

**Figure 23.** Views of Loweswater from the forest track

The peaks of Loweswater fell can be seen with their steep slopes plunging down to the north-eastern shores of Loweswater.

4.  Continue along the track, passing by another track that joins from the left. Soon afterwards, a pleasant ford is reached with the option of either crossing through or over it via the footbridge. Keeping to the left, pass the track on the right that leads to the stone hut.

5.  The trees begin to form a shaded canopy, providing the walker with a little respite from the sun in the summer months. Another ford is reached, again the luxury of a footbridge is provided for the less adventurous. With wellington boots, the ford can easily be crossed without getting wet feet; bringing much delight, no doubt, to the little passenger(s).

6.  At the edge of Holme Wood, a dry-stone wall is met that leads to a small wooden gate where further views of the lake can be seen. This marks the end of the route at which point the ATP can be turned round for the return journey back to the car park.

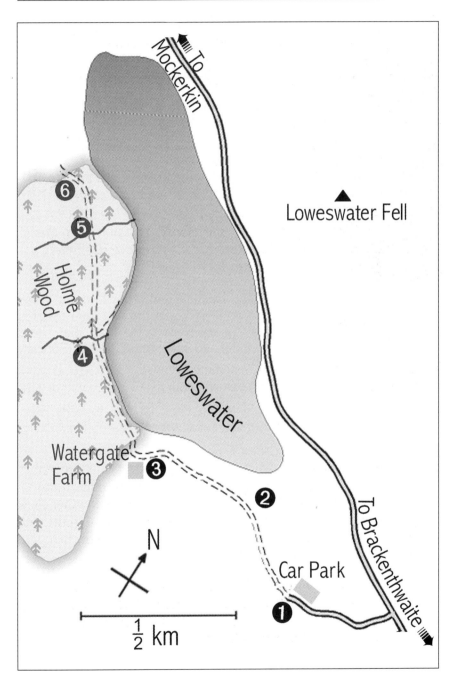

# Walk 21: Lowther Castle

*Lowther Park, with its gentle, well-manicured land, stands in sharp contrast to the rugged terrain of the central Lakeland. With a majestic castle taking centre stage, the route leads down to the River Lowther. Unusually, the downhill stretch is on the outward leg, saving all the exertion for the return. Definitely a route not to be missed.*

**Starting Point:** Travelling through Lowther park from Askham, cross over the cattle grid, leaving the park and take the first right towards Newtown. Park in the gravel lay-by 150m along the road, opposite a detached house with large wooden door signed "Lowther Forestry Group". (Grid reference: 526242)

**Distance:** 4km (there and back). Allow 2 hours

**Terrain:** Wide tracks. Relatively steep track leading towards river. Requires some exertion. The terrain is suitable for all-year-round walking.

**Maps:** Ordnance Survey Explorer OL 5 or Landranger 90

---

1.  From the car park, head along the road towards Lowther Park and away from Newtown. At the road junction, turn left into the park and across the cattle grid.

2.  Walk down the road, keeping to the side and looking out for cars for 150m. As the road through the park turns to the right, follow the track leading off the road to the left.

3.  Pass through the green gate and continue along the track towards Lowther Castle (see Figure 24). As the castle is

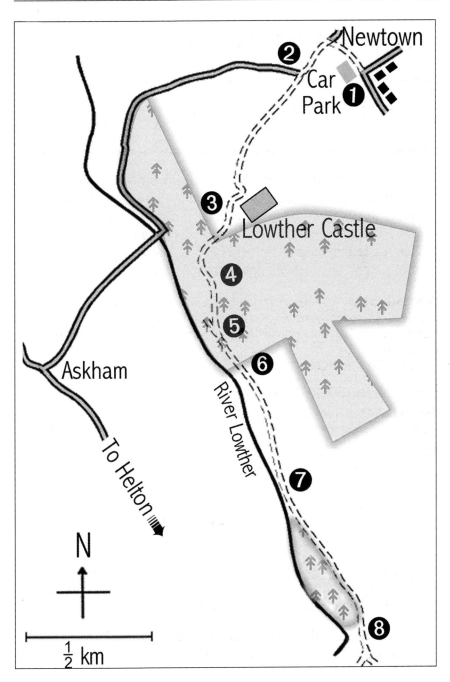

**Figure 24.** Lowther Castle

approached, pass through the metal gate towards the arches at
the entrance of the castle. The track turns to the right by the side
of the castle. Keeping the castle boundary walls to the left follow
the track around the right-hand side of the castle. Continue over
the cattle grid and then follow the track around to the left as it
enters the forest.

4.  Ignore the faint track to the left and continue downhill, keeping
    to the main track on the right. This is one of the few walks in the
    book where the outgoing journey offers the ease of the downhill
    stretch, saving all the exertion for the return.

5.  As the track begins to level out at the bottom of the forest a track
    is passed that joins from the right-hand side.

6.  Continue towards the river that can be heard before it is seen,
    passing out of the forest by way of the small green gate beside a
    larger gate. The track opens out onto large open farmland by the
    side of the River Lowther.

7.  Continue along side of the river, passing through a green gate running along a plantation with perfectly aligned trees, following the track on the right.

8.  Follow the track for another 0.7km, passing through the gate. After a short while the track leaves the side of the forest, before coming to a fork in the track. This marks the end of the walk. Enjoy the views and prepare for the exertion ahead as the climb back to the castle and the car park awaits!

# *Walk 22: Pooley Bridge*

*Pooley Bridge is a charming Lakeland village not far from Penrith and the M6 motorway. Situated on the northern tip of Ullswater, this route offers a gentle introduction to ATP walking. The route follows a river to the shore of Ullswater and passes by some fine examples of large old trees and, best of all, it is completely flat! At the end of the walk there are several gift shops to wander around and enough eating establishments to satisfy the appetites of even the most energetic ATP walkers.*

**Starting Point:** Travelling north, Pooley Bridge car park is situated on the right, just after driving over Pooley Bridge. Dunmalard Car Park is an alternative, situated on the left before Pooley bridge, although Pooley bridge will have to be crossed on foot to get to the start of the walk. (Grid reference: 471244)

**Distance:** 2km (Circular Walk). Allow 45 minutes.

**Terrain:** Tracks and bridleways. Crosses a grass field that may become muddy in winter. No climbs. Short stretch of walk on road.

**Maps:** Ordnance Survey Explorer OL 5 or Landranger 90

1.  From the entrance of the car park, follow the lane on the right between two sandstone gate posts with the sign, "Eusmere Lodge, Private Drive, Footpath only to lake". At the fork, take the right-hand lane.

2.  Follow the track to the green boathouse for the "Ullswater Steamers". Take the path on the right through a wooden gate between the boathouse and the lake.

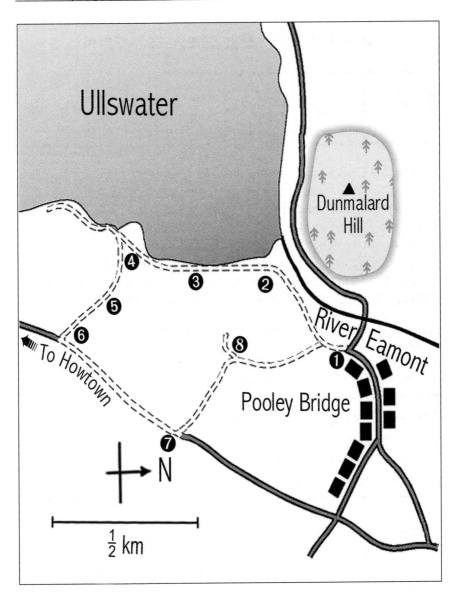

3.  The path follows a fence (see Figure 25) and, at times, the walker will have to negotiate open tree roots which, while being no obstacle for an ATP, can be slippery under foot.

**Figure 25.** A pleasant path following the lakeside

4.  After 5 minutes, the track approaches a small outcrop of land with a boat launching area. This provides a suitable spot for any children to paddle in the lake. After the break, take a left up the track leading away from the lake.

5.  The track enters Park Foot, an open-field campsite. Follow the track through the centre of the campsite field to the gate by the road. Views of Barton Fell can be seen on the right. An old Roman road crosses over this fell. This road is suitably named High Street – not for its banks & shops but because it is over 600m above sea level!

6.  Take a left along the road. While this is a quite, wide road, caution must always be exercised when walking in places where traffic may approach quickly and without much warning. A good example of a classic British hedgerow can be seen along the roadside. Follow the road for 300m, keeping an eye out for a wooden bridleway sign pointing left across a grassy field. Turn left here.

7.  Passing through the gate, the bridleway crosses a field with well cut grass but is not well defined and also may become sodden in winter. Head towards the white painted metal gate at the other side of the field to stay on the route of the bridleway. Some spectacular trees are passed in this field, with branches alone having the girth of many smaller tree trunks. As the white gate is approached, a wooden gate to its right can be seen. Go through this wooden gate.

8.  Take a right along the metalled road back to the car park and the delights of Pooley Bridge.

# Walk 23: Raven Crag

*Enjoy a walk away from the tourists and off the beaten track. With superb views of Loweswater and the precipitous Raven Crags, be amazed at where an ATP can lead! With a variety of terrain from solid wide tracks to narrow grassy paths, this walk has it all. A short section of quiet country road following the side of a gently winding stream completes this adventurous route.*

**Starting Point:** At Loweswater, take a right after the pub and then, at the tiny junction with a triangular patch of grass and black and white stripped post, take a right down the road sign-posted a dead end. Cross over the bridge and park in the parking are on the right.

**Distance:** 2km (circular). Allow 1½ hours

**Terrain:** Wide bridleway tracks, narrow footpaths. Paths will be muddy in winter. Some short, steep climbs.

**Maps:** Ordnance Survey Explorer OL 4 or Landranger 89

---

1. From the car park, continue up the hill on the metalled road. The hill directly in front is called Mellbreak, with Raven Crag also visible on its northern flanks.

2. After a short while, a farm is reached, at which point the road becomes a track. Follow it to the left of the farmhouse. The track steepens as it climbs the hill. Don't be afraid to take your time when climbing the hill as some wonderful scenery offers a suitable distraction from all the exertion.

3. Hemmed between two dry stone walls, the track levels out after

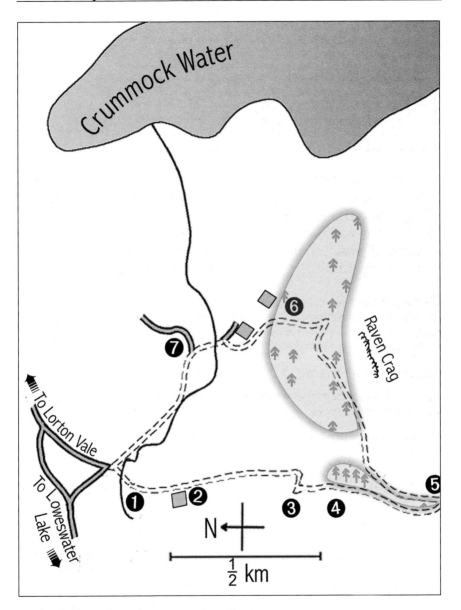

300m. The track turns sharply to the right, at which point Carling Knot can be seen reaching for the skies. The track turns again, sharply to the left, reaching a small forest.

**Figure 26.** The gentle track along the side of the forest

4.  Go through the gate at the edge of the forest. At this point, the energetic can race straight up the steep track ahead (pick up the route again at point 5). For those who prefer to conserve their energy, turn right and follow the track as it climbs along the side of the forest (see Figure 26). The track begins to flatten out as the dry-stone wall on the right leaves the track and drops down to the beck on the right. The trees continue on the left for a further 200m.

5.  As the trees on end, a pathway comes into view on the left. Take a sharp left, following this grassy footpath, travelling back along the other side of the trees meeting the "direct route" (see point 4) which joins from the left.

6.  Continue down the track, passing by Raven Crag on the right. The path can be wet and muddy in places. As the drystone wall turns abruptly left and drops down the hill, continue along the track in the same direction for 20m before, likewise, turning left

and dropping down the hill towards a house. Pass through the gate to the left of the house.

7.  Continue down the track between the dry-stone walls towards the next house. As the track becomes a road, turn left over a small hump-backed bridge crossing a stream and then left again at the next junction. Staying on the side of the road, continue for 300m, following the winding stream to reach the road junction by the pub, and return to the car park.

# *Walk 24: Rosgill*

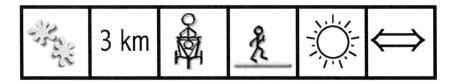

*Starting on the eastern border of the Lake District, this is a walk of contrasts. Beginning 0.5km east of Rosgill, the walk follows a wonderful track, lined with trees and dry-stone walls. At the end of the walk, a working quarry and the main west coast railway line is reached. Time the walk right and you could even see some high-speed trains travelling between Lancaster and Penrith.*

**Starting Point:** Rosgill Head, 0.5km east of Rosgill. Park on side of the road near the track exit so as not to obstruct other motorists. (Grid reference: 542169)

**Distance:** 3km (there and back). Allow 1½ hours

**Terrain:** Flat tracks and bridleway. Tracks can be puddled and are deep in places, so Wellington boots are the best option for footwear.

**Maps:** Ordnance Survey Explorer OL 5 or Landranger 90

---

1.  From Rosgill Head take the track eastwards; it is hemmed between two drystone walls. Follow the track round to the right, passing by the track that leads off to the left.

2.  Pass a small copse and go through a wooden gate; the track then bears to the left.

3.  Continue along the track for 0.5km, approaching the quarry. Go through the metal gate and follow the track as it bears to the right.

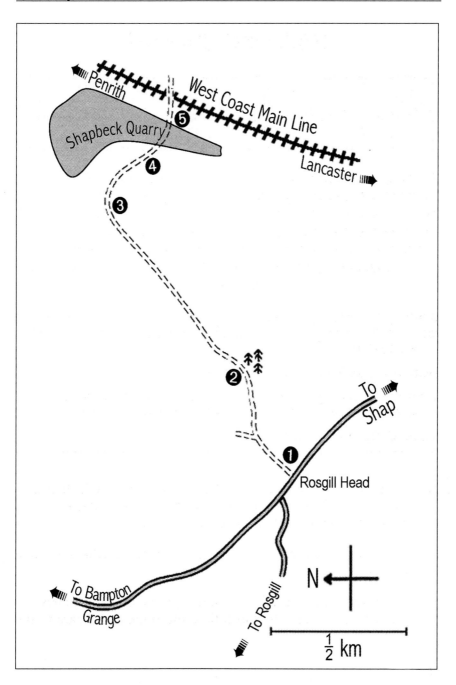

**4.** Pass by some small fenced ponds, and drop towards the railway cutting.

**5.** Pass through the wooden gate into the quarry, over a concrete bridge and the quarry railway track. Go through the next metal gate, leading onto the bridge that crosses over the railway line. With some forward planning and knowledge of the current timetables of trains travelling between Lancaster and Penrith, the splendid spectacle of a passenger train hurtling by may be witnessed. Returning along the same route, take in the scenery of the eastern Lakeland fells.

# *Walk 25: Steel End*

*This offers a walk in what would normally be impassable terrain for an ATP – marshes! The provision of decking, however, forges a trail through this marshy area by the side of Thirlmere reservoir. With superb views of the Helvellyn range of mountains, the walk offers a little more solitude in this quieter part of the Lake District.*

**Starting Point:** Steel End car park on southern tip of Thirlmere. (Grid reference: 320130)

**Distance:** 2km (there and back). Allow 1 hour

**Terrain:** Footpath and wooden walkways. The route is completely flat. Terrain can be wet and boggy in winter.

**Maps:** Ordnance Survey Explorer OL 5 or Landranger 90

1.  From the car park, go through the gate and over a beck, heading in the direction of Thirlmere. Looking ahead from left to right, the peaks of Helvellyn, Nethermost Pike and Dollywagon Pike can be seen, with waterfalls coming off their flanks. The path is firm to begin with, passing by reeds on either side – their presence indicating that the surrounding area is very wet and marshy.

2.  After 200m the path forks. Take the left-hand grassy path, ignoring the loose-stone path that abruptly finishes slightly further on. As the path begins to narrow, look out for Nab Crags, the prominent row of crags on the left. Walk over the marshy area on the wooden decking that can be very slippy when wet. The path

**Figure 27.** Views of Thirlmere from the track

passes by some trees whose roots have been exposed to the surface due to pathway erosion. These roots also can be slippy in wet weather.

3.  The path continues in a northerly direction keeping close to the lakeside (see Figure 27). Several more marshy areas are negotiated by way of the wooden decking; some sections of which stretch for over 20m.

4.  After about 0.7km of travelling northwards, passing through a number of drystone walls, a series of sheep folds is reached. These consist of a series of interconnecting drystone walls. Follow the path through the sheep folds, heading away from the lake to the small gate on the roadside. This marks the end of the walk. For those feeling strong, the ATP can be lifted over the gate to allow for a return along the road. Alternatively, the path can be re-traced back to the car park.

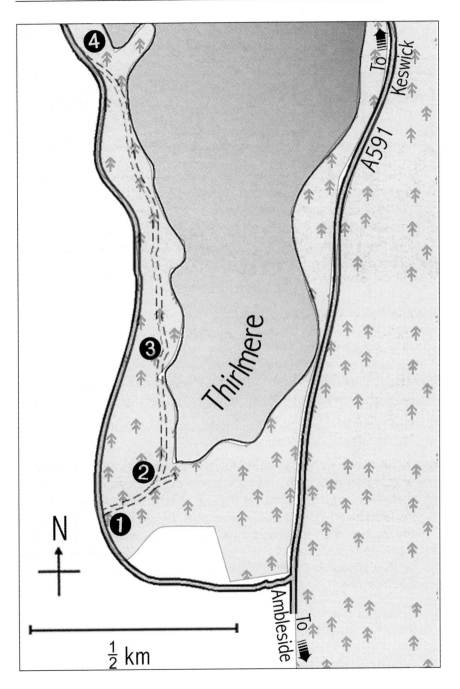

# Walk 26: The Swirls

*The Swirls is an aptly named car park with the wind seemingly hitting the walker from every conceivable direction. Fortunately, the route quickly takes refuge in the forest, on a wide firm track. Indeed, the forest not only protects from the wind but also obscures views of Thirlmere Lake. For those who don't mind occasional stretches of up-hill climbs, this all-year-round route is a navigational doddle.*

**Starting Point:** The Swirls car park is on the eastern shore of Thirlmere reservoir. The entrance gate to the track lies on the left-hand side of the lane just before the junction with the road. The gate has not been designed with ATPs in mind – and it will have to be lifted over before your passenger(s) can be seated. (Grid reference: 316168)

**Distance:** 3km (there and back). Allow 1½hours

**Terrain:** Wide forest track. Moderate ascents and descents. Terrain is suitable for all-year-round walking

**Maps:** Ordnance Survey Explorer OL 5 or Landranger 90

1.  Follow the track that leads in a southerly direction as it slowly diverges and climbs away from the road.

2.  Continue up it for 400m as the track bends around to the left (see Figure 28).

3.  Continue climbing a further 200m, passing by a footpath that joins the track from the left.

4.  The track then drops down-hill for 200m, reaching an open

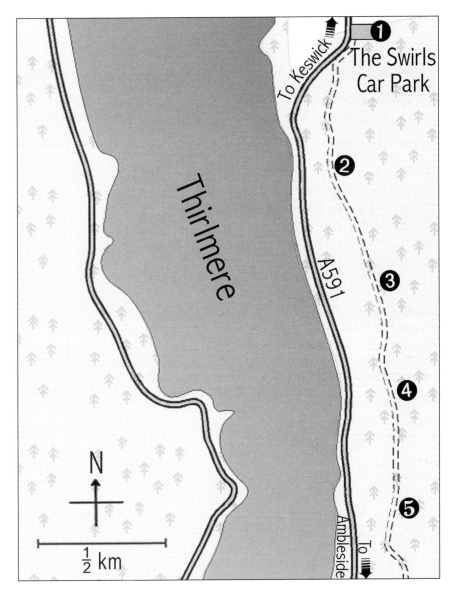

metal gate between the dry-stone walls either side of the track. Continue past the gate along the track.

5. Continue downhill until a closed metal gate is encountered. The

**Figure 28.** Seek protection from the wind along the forest track

track beyond is not open for public access. While a public right of way does exist along the footpath to the left, this is not suitable for ATPs. One has no option but to turn around and retrace the route back to the car park.

# Walk 27: Ullswater Ramble

*This is an exciting Lakeland adventure that takes in a ferry trip across Ullswater. Impressive height, magnificent scenery and a superb downhill run are the rewards for some initial sustained effort up a moderate to steep incline. This route should be tackled on a day with a good forecast because it is fairly exposed and the ferry trip puts an end to any last-minute turning back.*

**Starting Point:** Parking is available at Dunmallard Car Park. This is situated on the left, just before the bridge at Pooley Bridge. Secure at least four hours pay and display. Ferry departure times are at 10:00, 11:40, 13:55 and 16:25, although these are subject to seasonal variation. The 'Steamers' (which are, in fact, diesel-powered boats) run throughout the year, though winter sailings are less frequent. It is wise to confirm crossing times before kitting up the kids as they can change at short notice, depending on demand. The Steamers telephone number is 01768 482229 and the web address; www.ullswater-steamers.co.uk. (Grid reference: 469245)

**Distance:** 7km (circular, including ferry trip). Allow 4 hours

**Terrain:** Bridleway and tracks. Some lengthy climbs.

**Maps:** Ordnance Survey Explorer OL 5 or Landranger 90

1.  Turn right out of the car park. The ferry is 100m out of Pooley Bridge on the left. Catch the ferry to Howtown. The crossing itself is great fun and gives excellent views of Barton Fell on a clear day.

2.  After disembarking, walk straight down the track that leads

**Figure 29.** Looking westwards back towards Howtown

from the pontoon. Turn right along the road and cross a small bridge. Turn left at Howtown Hotel, taking the road to Coate farm. Continue up the road between a grey stone building and a white house. Negotiate a short, steep tarmac section and turn left at the fork to Malgard. The road is marked as being private.

3.  Cross over a stream and turn sharply, towards a greenish white house as the tarmac changes to gravel. Keeping the house, on the right, pass through the gate marked "Private Ground, Cyclists please walk". The footpath is denoted by a green and blue arrow.

4.  The path now gently ascends, following a wall on the left. It passes a house and two old stone buildings before revealing left views of Ullswater. A bench on the right provides a place to rest from the strenuous exercise. The path does not go through the next gate. Rather, it passes by and over a stream. A bridge and small waterfall (Swarthbeck Gill) on the right make for a lovely picnic site.

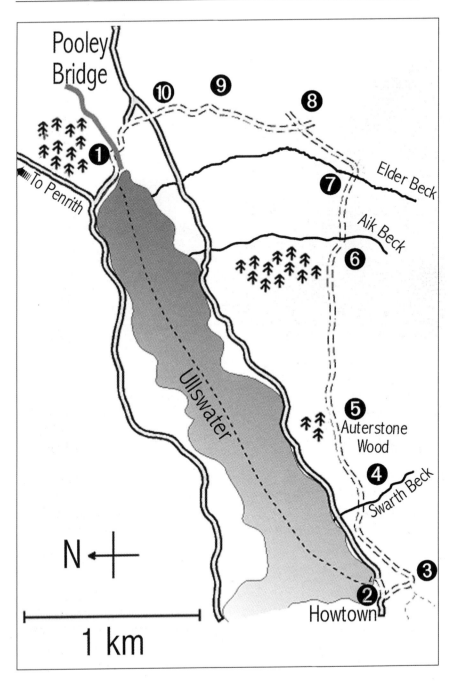

Pooley
Bridge

To Penrith

Elder Beck

Aik Beck

Ullswater

Auterstone
Wood

Swarth Beck

N

1 km

Howtown

5. Continue climbing gently for 0.7km, following the dry-stone wall on the left to the corner of Auterstone Wood. Here, the path starts to rise more steeply (see Figure 29) for about 1km, towards the corner of a forest (this stretch should take 20-30 minutes).

6. At the corner of the Forest the lion's share of the climbing is now complete – time for a well-earned rest! Continue along the track maintaining roughly the same height, and cross over Aik Beck.

7. The track remains flat for 1km and passes over Elder Beck. The track then bends to the left and goes down-hill.

8. After 0.5km take a left turn down the major track by a pile of white stones.

9. Follow the track for 1km to a metalled road.

10. Follow the road down to a junction (stay to the side as cars do occasionally use this road), and pass a caravan site on the right. At the junction, take the road straight across, back into Pooley Bridge for a well earned refreshment stop at the end of the walk.

# *Walk 28: Wet Sleddale Reservoir*

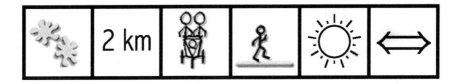

*Situated on the eastern side of the Lake District just south of Shap, Wet Sleddale reservoir was amongst a group of reservoirs created to supply water to the burgeoning population of Manchester. An area of diverse wildlife, this unique area of the Lakes is the breeding ground for a wide variety of birds. The walk follows the length of the reservoir along a well defined track – ideal for a short stroll on a sunny afternoon, even the most unadventurous will find this walk a breeze!*

**Starting Point:** Car Park at south-west tip of reservoir. Reservoir is sign posted from the A6, 2km south of Shap. (Grid reference: 554114)

**Distance:** 2km (there and back) Allow 45 minutes

**Terrain:** Wide bridleway track. Will be wet and muddy during the winter months

**Maps:** Ordnance Survey Explorer OL 5 or Landranger 90

1.  Follow the flat track on the left-hand side of the reservoir. After 50m cross over a tiny ford. Pass through the metal gate next to the style.

2.  At the fork, stay on track to the right, passing a track on the left which climbs a hill towards the barn.

3.  The track then drops slightly towards the side of the reservoir. Ford another tiny stream by the broken down dry-stone wall leading to the lakeside. Further on, a large boulder lies across the track that may require the ATP to be carried over.

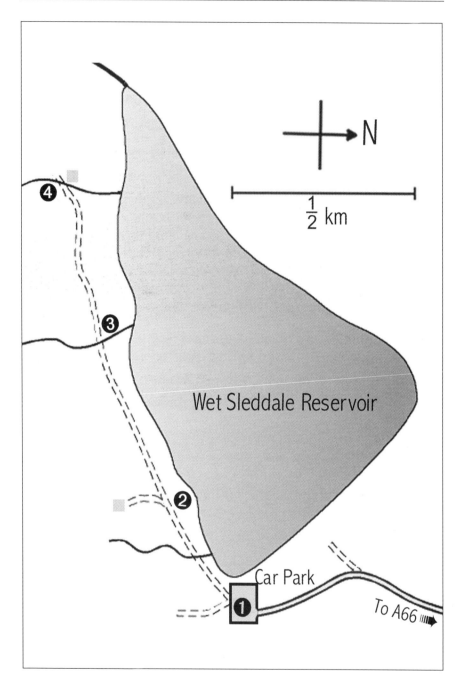

**Figure 30.** Wet Sleddale Reservoir

**4.** Staying on the track, a derelict stone house is approached. Pass through the wooden gate to the left of the house. Shortly afterwards a footbridge is reached. This marks the end of the walk.

# Walk 29: Whinlatter Forest Park

*With quick, easy access from Keswick, this route offers some superb scenery from the southern tip of Bassenthwaite Lake across to Derwent Water. A popular venue for mountain bikers, be sure to keep your eyes peeled – they can be seen before they are heard! For the more energetic walker, the route climbs to the lofty height of 400m, where the lightest breeze seems to have a more chilling effect. This is a good all-year-round walk with refreshments available next to the car park.*

**Starting Point:** Whinlatter Forest Park. (Grid reference: 210245)

**Distance:** 4km (circular). Allow 2½ hours

**Terrain:** Wide forest tracks. Steep climbs in places

**Maps:** Ordnance Survey Explorer OL 4 or Landranger 89 or 90

1. From the car park, re-join the road, passing the wooden buildings on raised land to the left, and proceed over the speed-bumps. A white cottage can be seen on the right. Just before this cottage is a track heading up into the forest on the left. A green wooden post with a purple arrow points the way in addition to a signpost indicating it is also a cycle route – a timely reminder to be vigilant for mountain bikers!

2. Climb the track until the gradient becomes more gentle, passing by a footpath that joins from the left before the track bends to the left.

3. Continue climbing up the track, passing by a path which makes

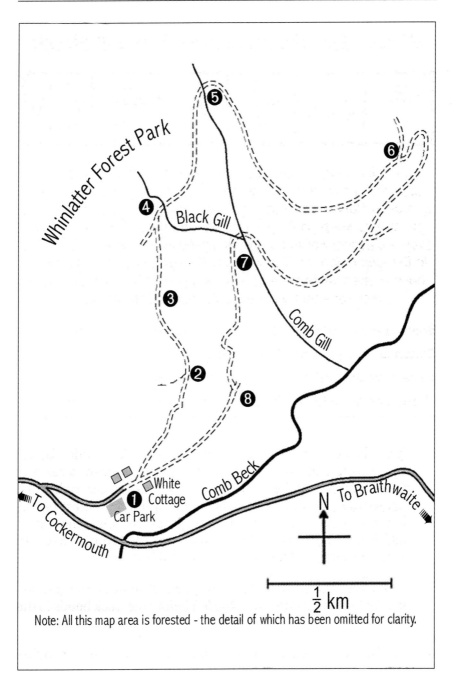

Note: All this map area is forested - the detail of which has been omitted for clarity.

**Figure 31.** Splendid views from the heights of the route

a hair-pin turn to the right. The track then bends to the right, continuing uphill.

4.  At the junction, take the right track, passing over Black Gill. This track climbs around the valley with Comb Gill running along its base.

5.  Cross over Comb Gill and, soon after, the highest point of the walk is reached. Views of Grisedale Pike can be seen on the right. Pass the track on the right with a post painted yellow on the top with a number 10 on it.

6.  Continue along the track, dropping downhill and around Comb Gill, to a junction. Take the track that drops to the right, ignoring the track that climbs to the left. The track bends round sharply to the right into a recently de-forested area, giving superb views of Bassenthwaite Lake (see Figure 31).

7.  Continue dropping down the track, past the exposed park bench, again walking around Comb Gill at a lower level, ignor-

ing any minor footpaths to the right or the left. Pass over Comb Gill again.

**8.** After another 0.5km, a junction is reached. Take the track to the right. The track continues for 0.5km before returning to the car park.

# *Walk 30: Whitewater Dash*

*This straightforward walk can be tailored to an individual's needs – a gentle gradient tracks to the start of the waterfall, followed by a short, steep section to the top. Parents can choose how far they want to go! The walk allows children to experience Lakeland views and a feeling for remoteness within a short distance from the car.*

**Starting Point:** Parking is available in a small lay-by at the start of the walk. (Grid reference: 249323)

**Distance:** 5km (there and back). Allow 2 hours

**Terrain:** Bridleway and gentle tracks. Steep last stretch to top of waterfall.

**Maps:** Ordnance Survey Explorer OL 4 or Landranger 90

---

1.  Start on the concrete bridleway that winds uphill with a moderate gradient. The path passes two hills on the left; Little Cock Up and Great Cock Up (no joke!)

2.  After about fifteen minutes, the bridleway forks. The left-hand fork continues as concrete towards the farm. Take the right-hand gravel track marked by a piece of slate "Bridleway via Dash Falls. Skiddaw House. Threlkeld".

3.  The path passes a small stream and buttress (Dead Crags) on the right and a valley on the left. Excellent views of Whitewater Dash can be seen from here.

4.  The route continues to wind uphill to a bridge, whereupon it

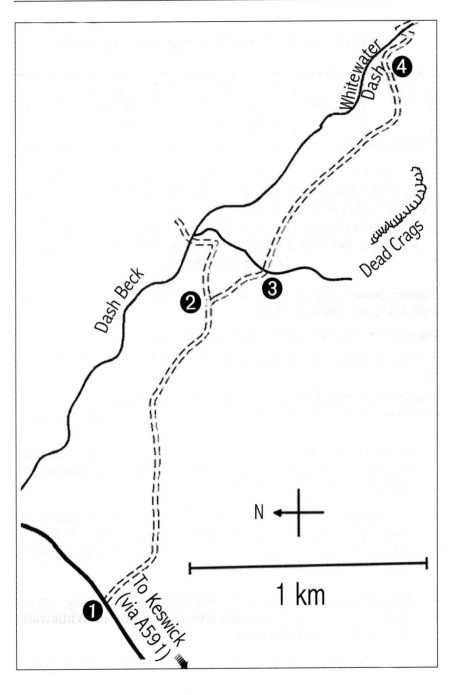

**Figure 32.** Views from the top of Whitewater Dash

levels out. An about-turn is appropriate at any point, although the fearless few who continue up the next hill will be rewarded with fantastic views from the top of Whitewater Dash (see Figure 32).